Keto Diet for Women

+

Anti-Inflammatory Diet Cookbook for Beginners

2 BOOKS IN 1

The Ultimate Guide for a Healthy Lifestyle After 60 with Tasty and Simple Recipes to Reduce Inflammation and Boost Your Immune System

By

MELINDA FRANCIS

TABLE OF CONTENTS 2 BOOKS IN 1

KETO DIET FOR WOMEN OVER 60

INTRODUCTION

What is the Keto Diet?

Before we get started, it is essential to clarify the keto diet. You've heard a lot about it, and perhaps you still don't fully understand what it is.

Here is a succinct and straightforward explanation of what the keto diet entails.

The ketogenic diet is a high-fat, low-carb diet with amazing health advantages, such as:

- weight loss
- help prevent Alzheimer's disease
- reduce the risk of heart disease/heart attack
- blood sugar control
- helps reduce high blood pressure

and so much more!

The Atkins diet and this one are both low in carbohydrates. However, with the Atkins diet, you progressively increase your carbohydrate consumption. The keto diet, commonly referred to as the ketogenic diet, calls for significant adjustments to your regular eating routine. This low-protein, high-fat diet severely limits all sources of carbs, including grains, bread, cereal, and many vegetables and fruits. While the keto diet may be difficult to follow, some people find that they experience benefits that exceed their disadvantages when they do. People over 60 may succeed on the keto diet because it may help with weight reduction, blood sugar regulation, and perhaps even heart disease prevention. However, there are risks associated with this diet. Therefore, you should always see your doctor or a qualified nutritionist before beginning any new diet.

What is the Principle Behind the Ketogenic Diet?

We already know it's a low-carb diet with high fat, but what is the underlying science or principle? By starving the body of carbohydrates, you make it burn fat instead of sugar, which causes weight reduction. But keto is more complicated than that. Its main purpose is to help people lose weight, but what about all the other health advantages? Women over 60 need to worry about it because it lowers the chance of heart attacks, may lower blood pressure and can help prevent Alzheimer's.

It's never late to start getting healthy, and the keto diet for women over 60 is an excellent place to start.

How Does the Keto Diet Work?

Usually, after consuming carbohydrates, your blood sugar rises, supplying the body's cells with energy. However, if you go without carbs for a long time, your blood sugar drops, and the liver starts using body fat stored as fuel. It's like a back-up system for your body. We refer to this process as ketosis. While on the keto diet, your body still has access to other energy sources, allowing you to keep your lean muscle mass.

Is Keto Healthy For Older Women?

In my experience, older women face various health issues or ailments. It's crucial to understand that what works for one lady over 60 may not work for another. When it comes to your health, please avoid comparing yourself to others. Keto is good for older women, but you should know that it's also not a very simple diet to maintain. It takes a ton of discipline and willpower, which I don't think I have much. We have been eating a certain way as older adults for our whole lives; thus, it will take a lot of work to alter that drastically, but it will be worthwhile.

CHAPTER 1

1.1 Ketosis 101

The Ketogenic Diet is one of the most popular and oldest diet plans out there. Although it has been referred to by many other names over the years, including banting, Atkins, Protein Power, and low carb, the concept is the same: limit your intake of carbs and sugars while consuming a reasonable quantity of protein and a lot of fat. If you are trying to lose weight or just be healthy, you've already looked into this diet, but there is a ton of conflicting information available, ranging from "OMG...this is the best thing ever!" to "eating all that fat will kill you". The keto diet consists of a low-carb, moderate-protein, and high-fat diet. This low-carb, high-fat (LCHF) diet encourages your body to use fat as its main energy source, which leads to weight reduction and a more constant energy level without the sharp highs and lows of a diet high in sugar.

Keto Diet For Weight Loss. Your body adjusts to the keto diet and starts using ketones from fat (instead of glucose from carbohydrates) as its main fuel source within 3 days to 1 week. Ketosis is the name for this metabolic process. When you reach ketosis, you use your body's stored fat and the fat in your food as fuel. Eating delicious fatty foods while losing weight thanks to your body's adaptation to become a "fat-burning furnace" is one of the key attractions of the keto diet.

Types of Ketogenic Diets. While there are many similarities across the many ketogenic diets that have grown in popularity recently, some significant variances should be acknowledged.

Standard Ketogenic Diet: The most well-known type of the keto diet, the Standard Ketogenic Diet (SKD), is exactly what we have just explained.

Cyclical Ketogenic Diet: The cyclical Ketogenic Diet (CKD) is popular among bodybuilders who want to achieve exceptionally low body fat levels for shows and competitions. A "carb loading" day is incorporated into the cyclical ketogenic diet (often once per week) to restore muscle glycogen and boost energy.

The Targeted Ketogenic Diet: Athletes who need more energy to go through strenuous workouts are drawn to the targeted ketogenic diet (TKD), which is more like the SKD. With the TKD, the person plans their carbohydrate intake to correspond with their workouts to satisfy their energy demands. You must slightly increase your protein consumption if you follow the High Protein Ketogenic Diet. In this variation, fat calories should make up 60-70%, while protein should account for 30-35% of calories.

Is The Keto Diet Safe? If you've looked up the keto diet on the Internet, you've run into a few articles that say it's harmful or risky. They exclaim, "Eating too much fat can clog your arteries!", "You won't get enough nutrients!", "All that protein will destroy your kidneys! "You must consume grains and sugars!", "Being in ketosis too long can be fatal!". The Framingham Study and the Seven Country Study are mostly to blame for the notion that consuming fats is unhealthy. The Framingham Study is a multigenerational study of residents of Framingham, Massachusetts, which started in 1948 and is still running today.

Dr Ancel Keys, an American physiologist who had conducted numerous other studies on how diet affected overall health, was the driving force behind the Seven Country Study, which took place between 1952 and 1957. This study focused on seven non-North American countries to examine the prevalence of heart disease in these populations. Both studies found that people who consumed more animal fat had a greater incidence of heart disease, but they disregarded other risk factors, including smoking and alcohol consumption. Although eating a lot of fat has been linked to heart disease, this link has not yet been conclusively established. While certain fats are seen to be healthier than others, the demonization of fat has significantly decreased over the past several years. Another bone of contention is the ketogenic diet's alleged deficiency in nutrients. Many people assert that cutting out grains, starches, most fruits, and non-green vegetables would result in malnutrition and believe that those following a ketogenic diet only consume steak, bacon, and cheese. However, many people who follow the ketogenic diet discover eating more veggies than previously. Moreover, consuming more meat results in more complete proteins and vital amino acids and nutrients like vitamin B12, zinc, and potassium. While it is true that eating too much protein might affect renal function, this only occurs when the kidneys are already damaged. As we noted before, extra protein converts to glucose, the fuel the body use first, which is why the standard ketogenic diet promotes larger ingestion of fat rather than protein. Going keto won't harm your kidneys if they are functioning normally.

Benefits of Going Ketogenic. While weight loss is the main benefit of the ketogenic diet, there are many additional advantages to adopting this eating routine.

Reduced Hunger + Increased Energy: You'll notice that your hunger is significantly less because you're consuming mostly fat and a small amount of protein, both of which are inherently satiating. This is because fat is a more stable and consistent energy source. Furthermore, you'll experience longer-lasting fullness and satisfaction following a ketogenic diet since fat is far more satiating than rapidly metabolizing carbs.

Improved Mental Clarity: Carbohydrates burn fast by nature, which causes sharp spikes in blood sugar levels. These spikes eventually culminate in a crash, which frequently leaves you feeling mentally foggy. Soon, all you want to do is return to baseline, so you reach for a coffee, an energy drink, or a candy bar. Once you start using ketones as fuel, you will soon notice an improvement in brain function, clarity, focus, attention, and problem-solving skills.

Accelerated Weight Loss: Chances are, this is why you are reading this book, right? By switching from glucose to ketones as your body's primary fuel source, you'll soon start burning body fat for energy, which will cause rapid and consistent weight reduction. This is not only a question of speculation or opinion. Scientific research has repeatedly shown that a low-carb ketogenic diet produces noticeably better outcomes than the conventional low-fat diet widely adopted decades ago.

Control Blood Sugar: Since you are cutting out high-carbohydrate and high-sugar foods (which convert to sugar in the bloodstream), many people notice lower blood sugar levels on a keto diet. The ketogenic diet has been proven to restore blood sugar patterns in people with diabetes as one is essentially avoiding the foods that cause blood sugar imbalances. Many doctors advise Type 2 diabetics to follow a low-carbohydrate keto diet to restore normal blood sugar functioning.

Higher Good Cholesterol: People are concerned with starting a ketogenic diet because they believe consuming more fat would negatively impact their cholesterol levels. Contrary to popular belief, low-carb ketogenic diets have been shown to boost HDL cholesterol while decreasing LDL cholesterol and triglyceride levels.

Reduced Risk of Many Types of Cancer: Cancer affects almost every household in the United States and throughout the world. Cutting processed foods and carbs, when combined with other forms of treatment, has been demonstrated to improve survival chances for some types of cancers.

Digestive Support: For people who experience persistent digestive problems, eliminating or drastically limiting carbohydrates can make a big impact. Many grains, starches, and sugars have been linked to GERD, constipation, and bloating in many individuals. Additionally, it has been suggested that fat nourishes good gut bacteria, improving digestion and stomach health.

Improve Cardiovascular Health: A high-fat ketogenic diet has been shown in studies to promote cardiovascular health, which may go against popular knowledge. This contradicts the "heart-healthy grains" claim that the American food lobby has propagated for years. Studies have begun to show that those who follow a low-carb diet (as opposed to a low-fat diet) have lower cholesterol and triglyceride levels and better cardiovascular health overall.

What Is Ketosis. Your body needs food to function, but different foods fuel your body differently. For many of us, a fast food breakfast sandwich, pastry, and sweetened coffee constitute a typical breakfast. This meal contains a lot of sugars and carbs, which turn into the simplest sugar, glucose, when digested. Before using any other fuel, your body will utilize glucose to power itself. You'll experience a spike in energy as a result of consuming this type of meal. Insulin is a hormone that transports glucose throughout the body for optimal energy. However, glucose burns quickly and hot, which is why you will feel "the crash" and the urge for another cup of coffee, candy bar, or pastry a few hours after eating. When your body cannot obtain glucose, it produces ketones, a fuel made from fat, and feeds on them. Ketosis is the state in which your ketone levels are raised; once you enter ketosis, you'll experience the benefits described above.

How to Reach Ketosis. Limiting your intake of carbs while increasing your intake of protein and fat is the simplest approach to raising your ketone levels. A ketogenic diet should ideally contain 60 to 80% fat, 20 to 30% protein, and just 5 to 10% carbohydrates. In comparison, the typical American diet recommends 300 grams of carbohydrates each day. A ketogenic meal plan would often have significantly fewer carbs than that, typically between 20 and 50 per day. A diet with less than 100 grams of carbohydrates per day is considered low carb.

Testing for Ketosis. There are various ways to check your ketone levels. The ease of use of ketone test strips contributes to their popularity. One is simply swiped through your urine stream while you wait a little while. The strip's tip will eventually change color. The darker pink the strip becomes the higher your ketone levels. For more accurate measurements, consider a blood glucose and ketone monitoring device, that is more accurate. This device collects blood from a tiny finger prick and provides the most precise blood ketone levels possible. Finally, we have breath ketone-level analyzers.

When you are in ketosis, you probably notice a metallic taste in your mouth since ketones are released in your breath. You will likely, at the very least, detect "keto breath," the unpleasant breath that ketosis is known to cause. This is caused by Ketones, which can be detected with a ketone breath meter. While there are other options, we haven't discovered one we love and highly suggest, so we stick with ketone test strips or ketone blood monitors. Of course, none of this is necessary to succeed on the keto diet, but it may be incredibly rewarding to observe physical indicators that you are in ketosis.

Tips for Reaching Ketosis. We'll go through a few things you can do to hasten the process by which your body enters ketosis.

Eat a Lot of Healthy Fat: You should restrict your carbohydrate intake and ensure you eat a lot of healthy fat. Remember, you should get most of your calories from fat. You'll also be less likely to go for a carb-heavy snack if you fill up on fat.

Keep Your Protein Intake Relatively Low: Remember that too much protein will be converted into glucose, the same thing that happens when you consume carbs. Try to limit the percentage of calories from protein to no more than 25% unless you're on a high-protein ketogenic diet. This implies that you can't eat a lot of steaks every meal.

Add Some Light Exercise: Studies have shown that exercise helps speed up the production of ketones. Indeed, increasing your activity level can aid in putting your body into a state of ketosis. We're not talking about strenuous, all-out exercise, just a little more movement. Walking is a good exercise almost everyone can do, or you can play your preferred sport.

Increasing Water Intake: Water is the ideal drink; while following the ketogenic diet, you should drink a lot of water. In addition to keeping you hydrated, water helps you feel fuller longer, which reduces your need for carbohydrates. Water has also been shown to hasten the removal of fat and ketones from your body.

Try Intermittent Fasting: Since a ketogenic diet reduces appetite, many people adopt a practice known as intermittent fasting. This entails limiting your eating window or missing a meal. For instance, you can just have lunch and dinner and forgo breakfast. While many believe it improves the efficiency of low-carb eating, it is not necessary.

1.2 Ketosis Vs. Ketoacidosis

If you have diabetes, you are undoubtedly well aware of the dangers of letting your blood sugar rise too high, resulting in diabetic ketoacidosis, or DKA. If neglected, this severe condition can become fatal. However, many individuals (including those with and without diabetes) may not be aware that a biological state called ketosis is similar and has nothing to do with dangerously high blood sugar levels and generally feeling awful. In-depth explanations of ketoacidosis, ketosis and the distinctions between the two states are provided in this chapter.

What is ketoacidosis? DKA, also known as diabetic ketoacidosis, is a significant short-term complication of diabetes that occurs when the blood turns acidic from too many ketones in the body in response to abnormally high blood sugar levels.

When no insulin is present in the bloodstream, the body cannot metabolize any glucose consumed, resulting in ketoacidosis. This causes a fast decline and needs urgent emergency medical care. Ketoacidosis can develop slowly over several days due to chronic illness and persistently high blood sugar levels or more quickly from a complete absence of insulin (caused by forgetting to take an injection before a meal or an insulin pump failure). People with type 1 diabetes experience ketoacidosis more frequently than those with type 2 diabetes. In fact, when type 1 diabetes is diagnosed, roughly 25% of people are in DKA. Even though it's uncommon, some persons without diabetes can develop ketoacidosis. Starvation, an overactive thyroid, or chronic alcoholism can cause it.

What are the symptoms of ketoacidosis? The following are some typical signs and symptoms of ketoacidosis. If you suspect you have ketoacidosis, please get emergency medical help right away.
- Extreme thirst and dry mouth
- Bodyache and headache
- Ketones in the urine
- Frequent urination
- High blood sugar
- Nausea
- Fruity-smelling breath
- Vomiting
- Weight loss (rapid and dangerous)
- Flushed face
- Blurry vision
- Extreme fatigue
- Confusion

How dangerous is ketoacidosis? Ketoacidosis must be treated right away by a medical practitioner due to its significant risk. If you believe you are in DKA and/or have moderate to high levels of ketones for several hours and cannot lower your blood sugar, call 911 or go to the nearest emergency department. Ketoacidosis can cause a diabetic coma and perhaps death if left untreated. Every diabetic patient should have access to at-home ketone strips to check for ketones in their body (through blood or urine) and help prevent the onset of DKA.

What is ketosis? On the other hand, nutritional ketosis is a physiologic state that happens when the body starts to use fat as fuel instead of glucose. The body can use the ketones generated when this fat is burned to produce energy. Rapid and sustained weight reduction can result from this (just like the weight loss seen at the diagnosis of diabetes, but this weight loss is harmless). This often happens when a person consumes a diet with minimal carbohydrates, such as the ketogenic diet, intermittent fasting, or (rarely) the Paleo diet. Nutritional ketosis can be reached after consuming 50 or fewer carbs per day for around 3–4 days.

Symptoms of ketosis. There are several signs that you could be suffering from the "keto flu" or the early withdrawal symptoms from sugar and carbohydrates, even though the only way to be sure if the body is in ketosis is to perform a ketone test.
These include, but are not limited to:
- Irritability
- Headache
- Brain fog
- Cramping

- Insomnia
- Constipation (and sometimes diarrhea)
- Elevated heart rate
- Dehydration
- Sugar cravings
- Muscle aches
- Nausea
- Bad breath (known as "ketosis" breath)

Drinking lots of water can help alleviate most ketosis symptoms entirely after a few days. Kidney stones are more common, a serious adverse effect that some people experience from long-term ketosis. A potassium citrate pill added to your diet can help prevent this.

Is ketosis dangerous? As long as your body has enough insulin, nutritional ketosis is safe for adults without chronic diseases and who are not pregnant. While in ketosis, a person can have normal blood sugar levels and not be in immediate danger. Women who are breastfeeding, trying to get pregnant, or already pregnant should avoid going into ketosis as it may reduce the amount of breast milk produced. Additionally, it is not advised for those who are going through the following to eat for a state of ketosis:
- Pancreatitis
- Carnitine deficiency
- Liver failure
- Porphyria
- Disorders that affect the metabolism of dietary fat

Long-term ketosis can cause low blood sugar, fatty liver, fatigue, chronic constipation, elevated cholesterol levels, and an increased risk of kidney stones in certain persons, although this is not guaranteed. Always talk to your doctor before starting any new eating regimen.

Can a diabetic person enter ketosis without being in ketoacidosis? Yes! Many people with diabetes follow a ketogenic diet and remain in ketosis while maintaining a normal blood sugar range, even though you should always consult your doctor before starting any new eating plan. In fact, several studies confirm the advantages of a ketogenic diet and maintaining ketosis for those with diabetes. People with diabetes who followed the ketogenic diet dropped an average of 26 pounds, according to two-year research.

According to separate research, the ketogenic diet increased people's insulin sensitivity by 75%. Staying in ketosis with a very low carbohydrate diet has even been shown to reduce hba1c levels in patients with diabetes if practiced for three months or longer. Always talk to your doctor before changing your diet or medicines because being on a ketogenic diet and/or entering ketosis might impact how much insulin and/or diabetic medication you need.

The key difference between ketosis and ketoacidosis. While the body produces ketones in both conditions, the mechanisms behind the production of ketones differ between ketosis and ketoacidosis. Ketoacidosis, a very severe condition brought on by ketones and inadequate insulin, can result in a diabetic coma or even death if untreated. It usually only affects those with insulin-dependent diabetes, although people with other forms of diabetes, an overactive thyroid, malnutrition, or alcoholism can also develop the condition. On the other hand, the ketones produced by the body in a state of ketosis come about as a result of the body utilizing fat as fuel rather than carbs, frequently as a result of fasting or eating a very low carbohydrate diet. If you have diabetes and are interested in learning how to enter ketosis, consult your doctor before making any dietary or pharmaceutical modifications.

1.3 What to Eat and Avoid on a Low-Carb Diet

It might be difficult to initially stick to a low-carb, healthy diet, especially if you're new to it. After you understand a few basic guidelines, you'll be astonished at how simple it is to follow the keto diet. Whether your objective is to treat a health issue like type 2 diabetes, Parkinson's, Alzheimer's, insulin resistance, or epilepsy or to lose weight, this fast guide to keto-friendly foods can help you make the best choices.

Which Foods Should I Eat on a Keto Diet? Keto Diet is about changing to a better lifestyle rather than merely trying to lose weight as quickly as possible. Contrary to popular belief, the ketogenic diet is not centered around cheese, bacon, and eggs. No matter how few carbohydrates there are, you should prioritize actual food and pay attention to its quality. Various whole foods, such as meat, fish, seafood, eggs, vegetables, nuts, full-fat dairy, and occasionally some fruit, such as berries, should be a part of a well-planned ketogenic diet.

Which Foods Should I Avoid on a Keto Diet? Your daily carbohydrate restriction on a traditional ketogenic diet will be 20 to 25 grams of net carbohydrates (or 30 to 50 grams of total carbs). Thus, you must avoid all high-carb items, such as grains (such as cereal, pasta, rice, and bread), potatoes, most legumes, sugar, and fruits. Additionally, processed meals and inflammatory fats should be avoided or consumed in moderation. A low-carb diet is simple to follow on our KetoDiet App. You'll discover hundreds of low-carb recipes, how-to articles, expert advice, and daily monitoring – everything you need to follow a healthy keto diet in one place. The most popular low-carb foods suggested for the ketogenic diet are listed in detail below.

EAT Freely:
- Grass-fed and wild animal sources: Grass-fed meat (goat, venison, beef, lamb), ghee, wild-caught fish and seafood (avoid farmed fish), pastured eggs, gelatin, pastured pork and poultry, and butter - these are high in healthy omega-3 fatty acids (avoid meat covered in breadcrumbs and sausages, hot dogs, meat that comes with starchy or sugary sauces), offal, grass-fed (kidneys, liver, heart, and other organ meats)
- Healthy fats: Saturated fats (chicken fat, duck fat, lard, tallow, clarified butter (ghee), butter, goose fat, MCT oil, and coconut oil)
- Monounsaturated fats: (macadamia oil, olive oil, and avocado oil)
- Polyunsaturated fats: omega-3 fatty acids, especially from animal sources (fatty fish and seafood)
- Non-starchy vegetables and mushrooms: Leafy greens (Spinach, lettuce, swiss chard, bok choy, radicchio, chard, chives, endive, etc.). Some cruciferous vegetables like kohlrabi, kale (dark leaf), radishes. Celery stalk, summer squash (spaghetti squash, zucchini), asparagus, cucumber, bamboo shoots. Mushrooms (Portobello, shiitake, white, brow, chanterelle, etc.)
- Fruits: olives, avocado, coconut
- Beverages and Condiments: Coffee (black or with coconut milk or cream), water (still), tea (herbal, black)
- Pork rinds (cracklings) for "breading"
- Pesto, bone broth (make your own), pickles, mayonnaise, mustard, fermented foods (kombucha, kimchi, and sauerkraut (make your own)
- All herbs and spices, lime or lemon juice, and zest
- Whey protein (beware of artificial sweeteners, additives, soy lecithin, and hormones), egg white protein, and gelatin (hormone-free, grass-fed)

EAT Occasionally:

- Vegetables and Fruits: Some cruciferous vegetables (green and white cabbage, broccoli, turnips, brussels sprouts, red cabbage, cauliflower, fennel, swede/ rutabaga). Nightshades (tomatoes, peppers, eggplant). Some root vegetables (parsley root), leek, onion, spring onion, winter squash (pumpkin), garlic. Sea vegetables (homburg, nori), okra, sugar snap peas, bean sprouts, globe or French artichokes, wax beans, water chestnuts. Berries (blueberries, blackberries, strawberries, mulberries, raspberries, cranberries, etc.)
- Grain-fed animal sources and full-fat: Dairy Poultry, beef, ghee, and eggs (avoid farmed pork, it is too high in omega-6 fatty acids). Dairy products (cottage cheese, plain full-fat yogurt, sour cream, cheese, heavy cream) - avoid products labeled "low-fat" because most of them are packed with starch and sugar that will only stimulate your appetite.
- Bacon: beware of added starches (nitrates are acceptable if you consume foods high in antioxidants) and preservatives
- Nuts and seeds: Macadamia nuts (high in monounsaturated fats, very low in carbs). Walnuts, hazelnuts, pecans, almonds, pine nuts, sesame seeds, sunflower seeds, flaxseed, pumpkin seeds, chia seeds, hemp seeds. Brazil nuts (beware of high levels of selenium – do not consume too many of them!)
- Fermented soy products: If eaten, only non-GMO and fermented soy products such as tamari (gluten-free soy sauce), paleo-friendly coconut aminos, or Natto, Tempeh. Edamame (green soy beans), black soybeans – unprocessed
- Condiments: healthy zero-carb sweeteners (Swerve, Stevia, Erythritol, etc.). Thickeners: xanthan gum (xanthan gum isn't paleo-friendly - some people following the paleo diet use it, as you only need little amount), arrowroot powder. Sugar-free tomato products (passata, puree, ketchup). Carob and cocoa powder, extra dark chocolate (more than 70 percent, better 90 percent, and beware of soy lecithin). Beware of sugar-free mints and chewing gums - some of them have carbs from sugar alcohols like xylitol, sorbitol, and maltitol that may increase blood sugar and cause digestive problems
- Some Fruits, Vegetables, Seeds, and Nuts with Average Carbohydrates: based on your daily carb limit
- Root vegetables: beetroot, parsnip, celery root, carrot, and sweet potato
- Watermelon, Galia / Cantaloupe / Honeydew melons
- Cashew nuts and pistachio, chestnuts

Only very little amounts, better avoided completely:

- Dragon fruit (Pitaya), apricot, peach, grapefruit, kiwifruit, nectarine, apple, kiwi berries, cherries, pears, orange, plums, figs (fresh)
- Alcohol: Dry white wine, spirits (unsweetened), dry red wine - avoid for weight loss, only for weight maintenance.

Avoid Completely:

- Food rich in factory-farmed meat, carbohydrates, and processed foods
- Foods with added sugar. Avoid sweeteners that increase blood sugar, stimulate your appetite, cause insulin spikes and kick you out of ketosis.
- All grains, even whole meals (oats, corn, wheat, rye, barley, sorghum, rice, amaranth, millet, bulgur, sprouted grains, buckwheat), white potatoes, and quinoa. This includes all products made from grains (pizza, cookies, pasta, bread, crackers, etc.), sugar, and sweets (HFCS, agave syrup, cakes, table sugar, ice creams, sugary soft drinks, and sweet puddings).

- Factory-farmed fish and pork are high in inflammatory omega-6 fatty acids. Farmed fish may contain PCBs; avoid fish high in mercury.
- Processed foods containing carrageenan (e.g., almond milk products - watch for additives), BPAs (they do not have to be labeled!), MSG (e.g., in some whey protein products), wheat gluten, sulphites (e.g., gelatin, dried fruits).
- Artificial sweeteners (Equal sweeteners containing Aspartame, Splenda, Acesulfame, Saccharin, Sucralose, etc.) may cause cravings and have also been associated with other health issues such as migraines.
- Refined fats/oils (e.g., cottonseed, canola, sunflower, safflower, soybean, corn oil, grapeseed), trans fats such as margarine.
- Low-carb," "zero-carb," and "Low-fat" products (diet soda and drinks, Atkins products, mints, and chewing gums may be high in carbs or contain gluten, artificial additives, etc.)
- Milk (only small amounts of raw, full-fat milk is allowed). Milk isn't recommended for several reasons. Firstly, milk is difficult to digest because it lacks the "good" bacteria (eliminated through pasteurization) and may contain hormones. Secondly, it's rich in carbs (4-5 grams per 100 ml). For tea and coffee, replace milk with cream in reasonable amounts. You may have a small amount of raw milk but watch for the added carbohydrates. Lastly, American farmers utilize genetically modified bovine growth hormone (rBGH). Dairy cows are given rBGH injections to boost milk production. Choose full-fat dairy products labeled "NO rBGH."
- Alcoholic, sweet drinks (sweet wine, beer, cocktails, etc.)
- Tropical fruit (banana, papaya, pineapple, mango, etc.) and high-carb fruit (grapes, tangerine, etc.) Also, avoid fruit juices (including 100 percent fresh juices!) - It is preferable to drink smoothies, abut either way very limited. Smoothies contain fiber, which is at least more satiating than juices, which are sugary water. This also includes dried fruit (raisins, dates, etc.).
- Avoid soy products primarily for health concerns, aside from a few non-GMO fermented products, which are renowned for their health advantages. Likewise, stay away from any wheat gluten that may be present in low-carb dishes. You should not eat any part of bread when you give up bread. Avoid BPA-lined cans. Use glass jars or other naturally BPA-free containers wherever you can, or create your ketchup, coconut milk, ghee, or mayonnaise.
- Legumes (lentils, peanuts, beans, chickpeas, etc.). Legumes, except peanuts, have a fair amount of carbohydrates and should be avoided. Legumes are difficult to digest due to lectins and phytates, in addition to their high carbohydrate content. They have been linked to Hashimoto's, PCOS, IBS, and leaky gut syndrome. Some people steer clear of peanuts, while others consume them in moderation

1.4 Benefits

The ketogenic diet has a range of health benefits:

1. Supports weight loss

2. Improves acne

3. Might lower the risk of some cancers (According to one study, certain cancer patients may benefit from using the ketogenic diet as a safe and effective supplemental therapy in addition to chemotherapy and radiation therapy. This is because it would kill cancer cells by inducing greater oxidative stress in them than in normal cells. However, additional research is required.)

4. May improve heart health

5. May protect brain function

6. Potentially reduces seizures

7. Improves PCOS symptoms

A hormonal condition known as polycystic ovary syndrome (PCOS) can cause an excess of male hormones, ovulatory failure, and polycystic ovaries. A high-carbohydrate diet can negatively affect those with PCOS, such as weight gain and skin issues. The ketogenic diet and PCOS have not been the subject of many clinical investigations. Five women were studied in one pilot research over 24 weeks in 2005. The researchers discovered that a ketogenic diet improved several PCOS markers, including:

- hormone balance
- weight loss
- levels of fasting insulin
- follicle-stimulating hormone (FSH) and ratios of luteinizing hormone (LH)

A different review of studies from 2019 discovered that patients with hormonal abnormalities, such as PCOS and type 2 diabetes, benefited from a ketogenic diet. They did, however, add a warning that the research were too diverse to suggest a ketogenic diet as a general PCOS treatment.

1.5 Risks And Complications

The ketogenic diet may have a range of health benefits. Long-term adherence to the ketogenic diet, however, may have negative health effects, including an elevated risk of the following conditions:

- excess protein in the blood
- kidney stones
- vitamin and mineral deficiencies
- a build-up of fat in the liver

Many individuals refer to the negative side effects of the ketogenic diet as "keto flu." These negative outcomes may include:

1. Constipation

2. Low blood sugar
3. Fatigue
4. Nausea
5. Headaches
6. Low tolerance for exercise
7. Vomiting

The keto diet should be avoided by some populations, including:
- Those with diabetes who are insulin-dependent
- Those who have eating disorders
- People who have pancreatitis or renal disease
- Women who are pregnant or breastfeeding

A ketogenic diet should not be adopted by people who use sodium-glucose cotransporter 2 (SGLT2) inhibitors, a form of medicine for type 2 diabetes. This medication raises the risk of diabetic ketoacidosis, a severe condition that increases acidity in the blood. Any proposed diet plan should be discussed with a doctor, dietician, or other qualified healthcare professional, especially if the person is trying to manage a health problem or disease. To make sure the keto diet is a safe eating pattern, those thinking about starting it should visit a doctor and disclose any existing medical concerns, such as diabetes, heart disease, hypoglycemia, or other diseases. Remember that there isn't enough research on the long-term advantages of the ketogenic diet. It is unclear if following this diet for longer periods is more beneficial than following less strenuous healthy eating habits. Carbs are severely restricted on a ketogenic diet. Some carbs do, however, provide health benefits. People should eat a variety of nutrient-dense, fiber carbohydrates.

CHAPTER 2

2.1 Why is Weight Loss After 60 Hard?

Let's face it; it isn't easy to lose weight after 60. You could eat whatever you wanted back in the day (for the most part). You consume a Hershey's Kiss and gain 2 pounds the next day. We lose the ability to consume anything we want as our bodies age. Suddenly, tracking calories and steps is necessary to beat weight. To understand why maintaining a healthy weight has suddenly become so challenging, read on for a list of 9 practical strategies to lose weight, remain in shape, and feel like you're 25 again. Although many people begin to experience this annoyance around the age of 60, losing weight and keeping it off can become a problem as early as 50. What is happening? Your metabolism is slowing down as a result of hormones. To begin with, as you become older, your metabolism decreases.

Robert Herbst on Losing Weight After 60: I'm 60; therefore, I understand what it is to be 60, says powerlifting expert and 19-time World Champion Robert Herbst. Loss of muscle mass results from decreased testosterone and human growth hormone (HGH) synthesis, which slows metabolism.

Carolyn Dean on Dieting After 60: Dr. Carolyn Dean, an author of 30 books, including The Complete Natural Medicine Guide to Women's Health, says, "Your efforts to lose weight are hampered because the loss of nutrients like magnesium has diminished the production of hormones that increase metabolism". In essence, you are not to blame for this. Age-related declines in your body's ability to produce essential hormones make weight loss a challenge. Perimenopause and menopause are common conditions for women in their 50s and 60s. You burn fewer calories due to this change than you previously did.

Jill McKay on Over 60 Diet and Exercise: "Our body temperature would change during menstruation, which would result in an extra 300 calories burned each month, says Jill McKay, a certified personal trainer, and group fitness instructor. Although it's not much, over time, it adds up. Insulin resistance is a problem that occurs throughout both perimenopause and menopause and makes it increasingly harder to lose weight". This means that you can no longer consume the foods you used to! This also applies to portions; you might discover that you can no longer consume as much as you formerly could without putting on weight. You Have More Free Time to Socialize – And Eat! There is more time when you are getting close to retirement. Of course, we would have more time to exercise, but is that really how we choose to spend our free time? Jill points out that elderly persons typically have greater possibilities for social interaction (and better finances to attend nice dinners). In fact, being among other eaters increases our propensity to eat more. It's challenging to maintain a healthy weight with all the socializing.

<u>Potential Health Conditions to Be Aware Of.</u> Most people find it difficult to lose weight beyond age 60, although this is normal. If, however, you are having difficulty losing weight, you might want to consult your doctor to ensure you are healthy. The two most frequent medical problems that might result in weight gain are 1) the thyroid losing function and 2) insulin becoming less effective. If you can effectively metabolize your sugars, you can tell by the hemoglobin A1c test that is commonly administered. If not, diabetes could be a possibility for you.

These disorders are especially prevalent in women approaching menopause.

9 Practical Ways for Weight Loss After 60. So many men and women struggle with weight loss after age 60. To tip the scales in your favor, there are several techniques for shedding that weight.

1. Strength Training: Resistance training, often known as strength training, isn't typically the first exercise older adults choose. The most popular workouts are often cardio exercises like treadmill walking or elliptical. Carol Michaels, an Idea Fitness Trainer, is concerned that many seniors are overlooking the benefits of strength training. Strength training is often the exercise component that's missing in weight loss programs for those over 60. This workout strengthens and develops muscle using weights (or your body weight). It strengthens muscle fibers and fortifies tendons, bones, and ligaments. We lose muscle mass as we age, primarily due to our slowing metabolisms. This leads to an even slower metabolism, and before you know it, you're caught in a vicious cycle. Strength training, however, may break that pattern of muscle loss; it can reverse muscle loss at any age. "Muscle is metabolically active; therefore, the more muscle mass you have, the quicker your metabolism," Carol explains. Strength training can therefore aid with weight reduction. But weight reduction is only one benefit of strength training. Additional advantages of strength training are:
- Better balance
- Less risk of injury
- Improved athletic performance
- Better agility
- Higher energy levels
- Better coordination

Another way to think about strength training, according to Robert Herbst, is that it causes the body to develop new muscle that is metabolically active and burns calories even while at rest. This new muscle raises the metabolism, just like a six-cylinder car uses more fuel than a four-cylinder one, even when idling at a red light. Essentially, you've broken the vicious cycle of aging and begun a weight loss and control cycle. Your increased muscle will help you burn more fat.

DO I USE FREE WEIGHTS OR MACHINES? Now that we are all in agreement that strength training is fantastic, you may ask how to do this. Many older adults, Carol claims, are in their mid-60s and have no idea where to start. Should you utilize the equipment at the gym? Do you need to purchase free weights? She continues, "While machines can be useful for people who have balance concerns, free weight exercise has several advantages. You can strength train at home with free weights and improve by one-pound increments. Using free weights teaches you how to move your body naturally throughout daily tasks. You can build more main muscle groups using free weights instead of a machine because you won't rely on them for support. Weight machines only work for large muscle groups. They can overlook the little but crucial stabilizer muscles that provide balance, coordination, and injury avoidance. Should I use machines or free weights in the gym or at home? Gyms offer free weights as well, so you have the option of purchasing your free weights or purchasing a gym membership.

DO I NEED TO STRENGTH TRAIN REGULARLY? Strength training sounds great, but if you think I'm going to devote two hours a day to it, you're mistaken. Not to worry. You don't have to strength train like a madman to reap the rewards.

Carol advises setting a goal of twice weekly. "Build up each muscle group, switching between your upper and lower body. To avoid creating imbalances, work the front, rear, and sides of the body. If you're over 60 and new to fitness, you could begin with a very light weight".

Strength training after 60. After you've scheduled your workouts, Carol advises performing the exercise 5–10 times. You should feel the muscle working around the fifth to eighth repetition. You should feel like you've exercised the muscle by the last repetition but not exhausted. If you are exhausted, you are doing too much weight. Many professionals online offer strength training plans with pictures and instructions, but you can call your local gym to have a personal trainer show you what exercises to do. Bodybuilding.com - do not be put off by the name - has a ton of pre-planned workout schedules. You can categorize them by length—4, 6, 8, 12 weeks, etc.—as well as by level—beginner, intermediate, and advanced.

2. Keep Carbs and Sugars Low: Even if you've never had a problem with delicious desserts and carb-heavy meals, dieting after 60 might be challenging because your body may start to change. Even if you've maintained your weight for years, that daily dessert can make you gain weight. The larger issue, however, is that older persons over 60 have a propensity for increased blood sugar because of insulin resistance. Functional Diagnostic Nutrition Practitioner Denny Hemingson, 61, explains that insulin tells the liver, muscles, and fat cells to absorb glucose from the bloodstream. When such cells develop insulin resistance, glucose is not used and stays in the blood, leading to excessive blood sugar levels. Eventually, this leads to metabolic syndrome, type II diabetes, and pre-diabetes. In this situation, the body finds it considerably more difficult to shed additional pounds. The solution? Reducing carbohydrates. Denny continues by stating that it's crucial to focus on blood sugar retention in people over 60 and that cutting carbs will lower your blood sugar, making it easier to keep a healthy weight. The Keto diet, which has high fat, moderate protein, and low carbohydrate composition, is supported by Carolyn Dean. This enables the body to burn down its glycogen reserves of sugar from carbohydrates before activating fat burning to use the remaining fat cells as energy. Although the Keto diet is steadily becoming more well-known in the health and fitness world as a means to burn fat more quickly than ever before, you are advised to see your doctor first. According to Carolyn, the Keto diet aims to limit your daily carb intake to 20–50 grams.

3. Drink Half Your Body Weight In Ounces of Water: Although drinking water doesn't in itself aid in weight loss, it's a fact that many individuals mistake thirst for hunger. The cure? Drink a ton of water. You should consume half your body weight (in lbs) in ounces of water, advise Carolyn and Denny. Carolyn says that people regularly mistakenly believe they are hungry when they are actually thirsty. So if you weigh 200 pounds, you must drink 100 ounces of water. That equates to 5–6 bottles of water each day.

4. Consider Adding Magnesium to Your Diet: You might not have considered including magnesium in your diet. Magnesium aids in synthesizing proteins, carbohydrates, and fats and boosts weight reduction and metabolism. Carolyn notes that in the 700–800 magnesium-dependent enzymes, energy production is the most significant enzymatic reaction to which magnesium helps. Adenosine triphosphate (ATP), the primary energy storage molecule of the body, is activated by magnesium. You may easily add magnesium to your water to add it to your diet. Add sea salt and an absorbable type of magnesium to your water, such as magnesium citrate powder, advises Carolyn.
This will make sticking to a low-carb diet much simpler and prevent you from experiencing the energy loss, sluggishness, and headaches brought on by electrolyte loss. Another thing to consider is that since sugar depletes magnesium and strains the body, avoiding it can help counteract the effects of stress.

5. Get Some Sun: Don't get sunburn or anything, but please take vitamin D! If you don't get enough vitamin D, you might reach for more food than you need. Leptin and vitamin D work together to control hunger signals, according to Denny. This mechanism breaks down when vitamin D levels are low, which makes people overeat. You can get the Vitamin D you need by getting more sun. Go outside, enjoy the weather, and celebrate your ability to restrain your appetite!

6. Reduce Stress Through Yoga: It is well known that stress can make us overeat. When you're feeling stressed, do you reach for some chocolate ice cream from the freezer? You're not alone. Relaxing is an excellent approach to handling stress. And occasionally, you require some encouragement. Yoga, which does more than merely reduce stress, is suggested by Denny. Your balance, core strength, and awareness will all increase. Consider using meditation, prayer, and nature walks as additional stress-reduction techniques. The Simple Habit application includes free, brief meditations that you can try if you are interested in meditation.

7. Get Quality Sleep: The impact of sleep on your general health is incredible.
You will have greater energy for your strength training session, and your body also creates human growth hormones while you sleep (HGH). Denny suggests obtaining 7-8 hours of good sleep every night. The greatest way to ensure that you get a good night's sleep is to:
- Establish a regular bedtime habit by going to bed simultaneously every day.
- Avoid using a screen before bed (smartphones, computers, TVs).
So don't skimp on sleep—it keeps you young!

8. Consider Meal Prepping: Meal planning can make you eat healthier throughout the week, even when you don't have time to cook (or perhaps you're simply not in the mood). Stop consuming manufactured food, Jill advises. Yes, this is difficult if you live alone. Consider meal planning for the week so you can prepare larger portions and divide them into smaller meals throughout the week.

9. Don't Push Yourself Too Hard: Lastly, try not to be so hard on yourself. If a week passes without you dropping a pound, don't worry! That could be completely typical. According to our experts, you shouldn't drastically reduce your calorie consumption. Don't substantially reduce your calorie intake, Jill advises. "Adequate calories are vital! Muscle loss brought on by rapid weight reduction alters body composition and may impede metabolism. In other words, if you aren't eating enough, all of your strength training success might be undone. Last but not least, don't overwork yourself at the gym. Jill elaborates on her own pet peeve: "One of my biggest pet peeves is when an unskilled personal trainer attempts to force a Baby Boomer to do a workout that is so difficult that they are so sore the next day that they can hardly brush their teeth or get up off the toilet. That's not necessary at all! If you need a break, take one! If you feel the weight is too much, lighten up! The goal isn't to make yourself miserable but to maintain your health.

2.2 Ketogenic Diet And Menopause

Menopause is the stage when a woman's menstrual period ends for 12 months in a row. It signals the end of her reproductive and fertile years. Common side effects of changing hormone levels during menopause include mood changes, hot flashes, and sleep disruption. Following menopause, many women also suffer an average weight increase of roughly five pounds. Some people suggest the keto diet, which has a very low carbohydrate intake and a high-fat content, to reduce menopausal symptoms and maintain hormonal balance. However, because it might have unfavorable side effects, it might not be the ideal strategy for all women. This chapter explores how several hormones might change while someone is in ketosis. It also looks at the possible advantages of this diet for menopausal women.

Keto and Hormones. Hormonal imbalances, particularly those involving estrogen and progesterone, can result during menopause. This can cause lower metabolism and decreased insulin sensitivity. Additionally, it could cause an increase in food cravings. There isn't much proof that the ketogenic diet can affect the ratio of reproductive hormones. However, the keto diet can significantly regulate the balance of certain hormones that affect insulin production and appetite management.

Benefits. Here are some potential benefits of the ketogenic diet for menopausal women.

Effect on Insulin Sensitivity: Insulin is a hormone that aids in transferring glucose (sugar) from your bloodstream into your cells to be utilized as an energy source. Hot flashes and night sweats, two symptoms of menopause, have also been shown to be significantly correlated with insulin resistance. Your body's cells develop insulin resistance when they don't react well to the hormone. This increases the amount of glucose circulating in your blood and increases your chance of developing a chronic disease. According to several research, the ketogenic diet may help persons with diabetes improve their insulin sensitivity, have lower insulin levels, and use fewer drugs to achieve their goal blood sugar levels. Additionally, one research tested the ketogenic diet on those with endometrial or ovarian cancer. According to the research, following the ketogenic diet for 12 weeks resulted in greater reductions in belly fat and increases in insulin sensitivity.

Effect on Weight Gain: People who are overweight or obese have been proven to benefit from the keto diet in terms of weight reduction, lipid profiles, and glycemic management. In one research, postmenopausal women examined four food regimens to determine which was most effective for maintaining weight. Researchers compared the Mediterranean diet to a low-fat, low-carb diet in line with the current Dietary Guidelines for Americans in the United States. At the study's conclusion, researchers discovered that those who consumed a diet low in carbohydrates, high in protein, and moderate in fat had a lower risk of weight gain. A low-fat diet, however, increased the likelihood of postmenopausal weight gain the most. It's crucial to note that the reduced-carb diet used in this study typically had 163 grams of carbs, which is significantly more than what is advised for a keto diet. There aren't many studies linking the ketogenic diet to menopausal-related weight gain.

Effect on Food Cravings: Many women report having more appetite and cravings throughout the menopausal transition and the postmenopausal years. It has been shown that the ketogenic diet increases feelings of fullness. For instance, one set of research indicates that being in ketosis may cause a decrease in hunger. This could be because of diets with a lot of protein and fat increase satiety through various mechanisms.

This includes decreasing intestinal transit, decreasing gastric emptying, and playing a role in releasing hunger hormones. Another research examined 20 obese people to evaluate their dietary desires, sleep patterns, sexual activity, and general quality of life while adhering to a very low-calorie ketogenic diet. Researchers discovered that patients experienced improvements in their sexual function, good eating management, significant weight reduction, and overall quality of life.

Side Effects. The keto diet may offer some advantages for menopause, but it is not for everyone. The "keto flu" is a common group of side effects that you may experience after beginning the keto diet. This is because switching to a very low carbohydrate diet requires some time for your body to adjust.

The following symptoms are linked to the keto flu:
- Brain fog
- Headache
- Body aches
- Feeling faint
- Stomach pain/discomfort
- Dizziness
- Sore throat
- Flu-like symptoms
- Fatigue
- Nausea
- Heartbeat changes

When the diet is carefully followed, symptoms often peak in the first week and progressively subside during the next three weeks. The negative effects that the keto diet could have on your general heart health are another issue. A few studies have suggested that a ketogenic diet's high quantities of saturated fat might raise the levels of low-density lipoprotein (LDL), or bad cholesterol, in our bodies. Diets high in fat have also been linked with inflammation and the disruption of gut microbiota (bacteria in the digestive system). Additionally, some people are concerned about the rigorous restriction on carbs, usually less than 50 grams. This is so because many items high in carbohydrates prohibited by the keto diet are also high in nutrients, including fiber, vitamins, and minerals. If you don't take the right supplements, you might be at risk for vitamin shortages. Menopause may be frustrating and difficult for some women, as can the time immediately after menopause. Know that you are not alone. Menopause-related weight gain can be lessened by adopting good eating habits and frequent exercise routines. Although the keto diet may help some people's symptoms, it's not a one-size-fits-all solution. Finding out which eating strategy will work best for you requires a conversation with your healthcare physician and a qualified dietitian.

2.3 Mistakes Beginners Make and How to Avoid Them

Given the paucity of data on the ketogenic diet, it might be difficult to predict whether or not you will have any specific effects, such as weight reduction. It can be challenging to follow the keto diet "properly" because it is so severely restrictive. For instance, you'll have to forgo starchy vegetables, limit fruits, and avoid grains, sauces, juice, and sweets on this diet. Moreover, as per the standard keto food list, you must consume a lot of fats (lots of them). By doing this, you'll enter the metabolic state of ketosis, which causes your body to burn fat instead of carbs, potentially increasing your weight loss.

However, because fats exist in various forms (not all healthy) and carbohydrates are present in almost everything, it may be easy to err here, especially if you're new to the keto diet. To ensure you're using this technique as safely as possible, avoid the following common keto pitfalls:

1. Cutting Your Carbs and Increasing Your Fat Too Much Too Quickly: You might be eating cereal, sandwiches, and spaghetti one day and then decide to start the keto diet and limit your daily carbohydrate intake to 20 grams (g), which is usually the suggested starting point. (For reference, a medium apple provides 25 g of carbohydrates.) That can be a major adjustment for your body. Consider easing in. According to Lara Clevenger, a ketogenic dietitian-nutritionist, "before starting a keto diet, individuals may benefit from weaning down their carbohydrate consumption instead of reducing carbohydrates cold turkey."

2. Not Drinking Enough Water on Keto: For all the attention on what you are eating, don't overlook what you're drinking. On a ketogenic diet, dehydration is more likely to occur. "Your fluid and electrolyte balance may change due to the ketogenic diet's significant reduction in carbohydrate intake". According to Alyssa Tucci, RDN, nutrition manager at Virtual Health Partners in New York City, "carbs are stored in the body together with water, so when these reserves are depleted, that water is lost along with them. She further claims that the removal of the accumulated ketones in urine by the body depletes it of salt and water. All that to say: Drink up. All of this to say: Cheers! To meet the recommendation of drinking half your body weight in ounces of water each day, Tucci advises waking up to a large glass of water and sipping on it frequently throughout the day.

3. Failing to prepare for the keto flu: During the first two weeks of the keto diet, you may suffer what is known as the "keto flu," or flu-like symptoms (such as muscular cramps, nausea, pains, and exhaustion), as your body switches from being a carbohydrate burner to a fat burner. Please note that not everyone experiences it. If you're not ready for this feeling, you could assume something is wrong and stop your diet altogether. More than that, according to Clevenger, planning your meals or meal preparation can help you get through the low-energy phase of the transition. She also suggests drinking plenty of water, consuming meals high in potassium, magnesium, and sodium, and other measures to deal with keto flu symptoms.

4. Forgetting to Consume Omega-3 Fatty Acid-Rich Foods: Don't limit yourself to bacon, cheese, and cream, even if fat is the main component of the diet. Aim to consume more anti-inflammatory omega-3 fatty acids, especially EPA and DHA, which are present in foods like salmon, herring, sardines, oysters, and mussels, adds Clevenger. (If seafood isn't your thing, try krill oil or cod liver oil.) If you haven't loaded up on avocado, olive oil, and seeds like chia and flaxseed, do so. Other healthy fats are also a wonderful option. Not only are they keto-friendly, but they also provide the beneficial polyunsaturated and monounsaturated fats your body needs to function at its peak.

5. Not adding enough salt to your food: Given that people consume more sodium than ever in a diet high in processed foods, you probably aren't used to hearing the recommendation to consume more salt. However, it's essential for keto. Not only does the body lose sodium when ketones are cleared from the body, but you may also consume significantly less table salt now that you've eliminated the main source of salt in the typical American diet: packaged, processed foods like bread, crackers, cookies, and chips.

Table salt is made up of 40% sodium and 60% chloride. "If you're on a ketogenic diet, chances are you'll need to make most, if not all, of your meals and snacks from scratch, so simply season with salt," Tucci advises.

6. Going It Alone and Not Clearing the Diet With Your Doc: Many people try the ketogenic diet, hoping it will treat a medical condition. If that is you, Clevenger advises that you first consult your physician to get their approval of your plan, particularly if you are also on medication. As your signs and symptoms improve, your doctor may need to change certain drugs," she adds. An example is insulin, which may require a lower dosage given your strict carbohydrate restriction.

7. Ignoring your intake of vegetables: Veggies contain carbs. You must thus be careful with how much food you consume, even lettuce. You risk consuming too many carbohydrates if you're careless or eating them randomly, which will cause you to exit ketosis. On the other hand, if keeping track of every small carrot becomes too challenging, you may skip vegetables altogether. But while watching amounts and properly tracking carbohydrates, it's vital to include veggies because they contain fiber that helps avoid constipation, a possible side effect of the keto diet. Choose nonstarchy foods in a rainbow of colors for a range of nutrients, advises Tucci, like leafy greens, broccoli, cauliflower, cucumber, tomato, asparagus, and bell peppers.

8. Getting Obsessed with Carb Counting and Ignoring the Importance of Food Quality: When significantly reducing carbohydrates seems to be the only purpose of the keto diet, everything else may seem like an afterthought. "Reducing your carbohydrate consumption is important, but when finances allow, focusing on higher-quality items can help enhance your health, too," claims Clevenger. This entails choosing foods high in omega 3, such as wild salmon, organic meats, or grass-fed, local, and choosing whole foods for snacks rather than prepared keto-friendly items. It also involves including as many nutrient-dense fruits and vegetables in your diet as you can to maintain a balanced diet. Many qualified dietitians aren't fans of the keto diet because it could result in dietary deficits. You can prevent these by working with an RD personally as you follow the keto diet.

CHAPTER 3

3.1 Keto And Exercise

Before you begin combining keto with exercise, there are a few key points that experts want you to be aware of. You've heard of the ketogenic (also known as the keto) diet by now; you know, the one that pushes you to consume a lot of healthy fats while largely avoiding carbohydrates. The keto diet has entered the mainstream and is especially well-liked by the fitness crowd. It was formerly used to treat people with epilepsy and other significant health conditions. While it's true that it may have some performance advantages, doctors say there are certain crucial facts you should be aware of if you're considering going out while on the ketogenic diet. At first, you might not feel so great. Naturally, not feeling your best might affect your workouts. Ramsey Bergeron, a keto athlete and NASM-certified personal trainer in Scottsdale, Arizona, says the first few days may seem like you're in a fog. "Your brain uses glucose (from carbohydrates) as its main energy source, so switching to ketone bodies produced by the liver's breakdown of fats would require some getting used to," he explains. Fortunately, the mental fog usually fades after a few days. Bergeron advises against exercising in dangerous situations that call for rapid reactions, such as riding a bike on the road with cars or taking a strenuous, prolonged outdoor hike. It's not a good idea to undertake a new workout during the first few weeks of a keto diet. It's not a good idea to sign up for that new boot camp class you've wanted to take if you recently switched to a keto diet. Bergeron advises, "Keep doing what you are doing." This is mainly due to the first point: most people don't first feel great on keto. When extreme, this initial unpleasant phase—which typically passes within a few days to a couple of weeks—can be referred to as the "keto flu" due to its flu-like grogginess and gastrointestinal disturbances. However, it is probably not the time to try a new class or aim for a PR. "When my clients try anything new, I always advise them to keep the variables to a minimum," says Bergeron. "You won't know what worked and what didn't if you alter too many things at once," he continues.

It's essential that you eat enough before exercising while following a ketogenic diet. "Make sure you're providing your body with enough energy, and avoid decreasing calories too strictly," advises Lisa Booth, R.D.N., a nutritionist and Nori Health's health lead. This is significant because, according to her, people on the keto diet tend to undereat. According to Booth, a keto diet also has an appetite-suppressing effect, so you can think you're not hungry even if you aren't providing your body with enough energy.

"When you restrict an entire food category (in this case, carbohydrates), you often automatically decrease calories," she adds. You'll feel awful if you drastically cut calories while working out, which might affect your performance and results.

Low- and moderate-intensity workouts can help you burn more fat. This is one of the key arguments favoring keto for weight reduction. "When you're in ketosis, you don't use glycogen as an energy source," says Booth. "Glycogen is a substance stored in muscles and tissues as a reserve of carbs. Instead, you're using ketone bodies and fat. A ketogenic diet can help enhance fat oxidation, spare glycogen, produce less lactate, and use less oxygen if you engage in aerobic workouts like biking or running," she clarifies. In other words, that may result in more fat being burnt during aerobic exercise. Booth continues, "But it probably won't improve performance". Furthermore, while following a ketogenic diet, you don't have to exert yourself to the fullest. According to Chelsea Axe, D.C., C.S.C.S., a certified strength, and conditioning specialist in Nashville, "Studies have indicated that ketogenic diets combined with moderate-intensity exercise can favorably impact one's body composition. Research has shown that ketogenic diets increase the body's capacity to burn fat both at rest and during low- to moderate-intensities, so your weight-loss efforts may be optimized when exercising in these zones," she says.

High-intensity exercises may be best avoided while on a diet. According to Axe, studies have shown that diets heavy in a certain macronutrient, such as fat, encourage a greater capacity to use that macronutrient as fuel. However, she says, "regardless of your macronutrient ratio consumption, the body adjusts to using glycogen as fuel during high-intensity activity. You'll recall from earlier that carbs fuel glycogen stores, so if you don't consume a lot of them, your ability to execute higher-intensity exercise can be compromised. Instead, Axe argues that moderate exercise is best for maximizing the body's capacity to burn fat. As a result, those who participate in intense exercises like CrossFit or HIIT might benefit more from adopting a ketogenic diet during their off-season or when they are less concerned with their performance.

To profit from your workouts, you need to eat adequate fat. This is essential; otherwise, you risk losing out on all the advantages and having your performance deteriorate. According to Bergeron, if you follow a ketogenic diet but don't consume enough fats, you are effectively following an Atkins diet with high protein, low carbs, and low fat. He says that doing so might make you incredibly hungry, reduce muscle mass, and be almost impossible to maintain. Most low-carb diets have a bad reputation for a reason. You're likely to experience fatigue and lose out on entering ketosis if you don't consume enough fat to make up for the carbs you're missing. According to Bergeron, most calories must come from good fat sources like fish, grass-fed meats, coconut oil, and avocado.

When combining diet with exercise, paying attention to your body is important. This is true throughout your whole experience, but particularly in the first few weeks, you follow a ketogenic diet. According to Booth, "if you often feel tired, lightheaded, or drained, your body may not function properly on a very low-carb diet. "The most crucial factor should be your health and wellbeing. See how you feel after adding more carbohydrates. If this makes you feel better, the ketogenic diet might not be the best option for you," she suggests.

3.2 Keto-Friendly Drinks

What makes a drink keto? Because the keto diet calls for getting fewer than 10% of your daily calories from carbs—roughly 20 to 30 grams a day—you should avoid drinks that exceed, or even better, fall well below, that percentage. Why? With very few exceptions, you don't want to consume all of your daily carbohydrate allowance in a single serving. When searching for keto-friendly options, look for beverages with less than 5 grams of carbohydrates on the nutrition label. Avoid heavily sweetened beverages (sorry, orange juice fans) or include additional sweeteners, which, regrettably, include most cocktails.

What beverages work best for a keto diet? We searched for the most acclaimed and highly rated keto-friendly beverages for this list. Some choices are apparent (hello, number one), while others will have you rushing to Starbucks to get every keto-friendly beverage they offer. To ensure that you don't feel like you are missing out on anything, we have also provided several alcoholic alternatives and soda substitutes. Before beginning the keto diet, consult a nutritionist and/or a doctor to ensure you're obtaining all the necessary nutrients. Do whatever seems right for you as well! All bodies are different.

Water. Yes, of course, we do. But water satisfies a keto-friendly substance's fundamental and most important condition: it contains little carbohydrates. Craig Clarke says on the keto site Ruled.me, "During the first few days of carbohydrate restriction, the body normally eliminates water and minerals at an accelerated pace. A few days later, when ketone levels rise, even more water than usual will be expelled." So drink up!

Sparkling Water. According to the aforementioned logcv, all zero-calorie seltzers are also keto. That means quitting your favorite La Croix habit won't be necessary if you go keto. The Sparkling Ice waters are also a favorite among many keto dieters. This Amazon reviewer wrote, "I'm on the keto diet and drink them constantly while still losing weight. They have a terrific flavor and satisfy my thirst. Additionally, each bottle has 0 calories and 0 or 5 carbohydrates."

Zevia Zero Calorie Soda. This keto-friendly Tiktok designer vouch for Zevia, saying, "If you are a soda-holic, Zevia is a wonderful solution to replace all that soda." Amazon shoppers adore it as a soda substitute because it contains neither calories nor sugar. Most diet sodas are also OK when following a ketogenic diet.

Green Tea. While on the keto diet, remember your body's other health requirements! Green tea adheres to the diet while providing much-needed antioxidants and minerals. Matcha powder is also included in this. According to Carine Claudepierre of the keto-focused SweetAsHoney blog, the ingredient comprises dried green tea leaves that have been crushed into green tea powder. It is carb-free and keto-friendly.

Black Tea. Black tea has no net carbohydrates, although heavy cream can be added for taste if desired, which is, in fact, keto-friendly. Tea is a good keto-friendly beverage because it's a perfect substitute for water and can be served hot or cold, according to the MunchMunchYum blog.

Bulletproof Coffee. Yes, you can drink your coffee black, but adding that sweet, sweet (but low-carb, high-fat) butter can help you reach your calorie targets much more quickly. According to a blog article by WholesomeYum's Maya Krampf, "Bulletproof coffee is coffee brewed with either butter or ghee AND coconut oil or MCT oil. My favorite part is the extra energy I got from combining butter and MCT oil with my coffee. I usually feel satisfied after eating it and am attentive and productive."

Non-Dairy Milk Alternatives. Protein. Fat. Little carbohydrates. Everything is fine. Almond milk, according to Elana Amsterdam of Elana's Pantry, is the greatest milk for the keto diet. It has amazing flavor and mouthfeel and is relatively low in carbohydrates, making it my favorite."

Protein Shakes. Now that everyone is interested in going keto, several protein powders are made expressly for the keto diet. You may either make your own or choose an Atkins-style shake. It has almost 23,000 five-star ratings on Amazon, and one reviewer claimed that it doesn't taste like "a 'diet' item". "I use this to satisfy my weet tooth craving while on the keto diet."

Hard Liquor. The blog Green and Keto claimed that "alcohols like vodka, scotch, rum, whiskey, gin, and tequila are great options on the keto diet. They have no carbohydrates or sugar when eaten alone". Just be careful not to combine them with any liquids or calorie sweeteners. Your best friends in keto mixers are sugar-free sodas, seltzers, and tonics.

Starbucks' Peach Citrus White Tea. After the drink became quite popular, there was considerable disagreement about whether it was keto-friendly, but in reality, it is. Only Starbucks' unsweetened Peach Citrus White Tea, heavy cream, two to four pumps of sugar-free vanilla syrup, and ice are combined to make it. All of those things are in the (keto) clear. A few low-carb blogs have even created versions of their recipes you can make at home.

Starbucks Pink Drink. The OG Pink Drink wasn't originally keto, but early adopters of the diet quickly figured out how to make it such. To give this drink a keto makeover, request a sugar-free syrup, unsweetened Passion Tango tea, and light or heavy creamer. "Grammable keto," boom. This TikTok creator said, "It is one of my favorite clean keto Starbucks beverages.

Lagunitas Daytime IPA. This beer has an ABV of 4%, fewer than 100 calories, and 3 grams carbohydrates. This indicates that it is keto-friendly, and the designer of the keto Tiktok claims that it has a "cool name" and "tastes amazing."

Michelob Ultra Beer. "Michelob Ultra is below 3 g carbs per serving and has 95 calories," Joe Duff of The Diet Chef wrote in a blog post. "It has a refreshing flavor with a little bit of sweetness."

CHAPTER 4

Recipes

Breakfast

1. Banana Keto Chia Pudding

Servings: 1   **Preparation time:** 130 minutes
Ingredients
- White Yoghurt - 2 tablespoons
- Chia seeds - 1, 5 tbsp
- KetoDiet protein drink banana flavor - 1
- Milk - 150 ml

Instructions. Mix all the ingredients together, pour the mixture into a glass and let it solidify in the refrigerator for at least 2 hours. Decorate with a sprig of mint, for example.

---

2. Green Keto Smoothie

Servings: 1   **Preparation time:** 15 minutes
Ingredients
- Fresh baby spinach - 30 g
- Apple - 1/2 pcs
- KetoDiet Protein Drink - 1 serving
- Coconut milk - 200 ml
- Young barley - 1 teaspoon
- Water - 100 ml

Instructions. Pour the milk into a blender, add sliced apple, baby spinach, water, protein drink, and young barley and mix all the ingredients thoroughly. Garnish the smoothie with a slice of lemon and serve.

---

3. Matcha Keto Pudding

Servings: 1   **Preparations:** 60 minutes
Ingredients
- Matcha tea - 1 teaspoon
- Chia seeds - 20 g
- KetoDiet protein panna cotta - 1 serving
- Almond milk - 100 ml
- Nuts mix for decoration
- Vanilla essence according to taste

Instructions. Mix the powder from the protein panny cotty bag and matcha tea into the almond milk, add the chia seeds, and mix the vanilla essence. Pour into a bowl and let it solidify in the refrigerator for at least 45 minutes. Garnish the protein matcha pudding with chopped nuts and serve.

4. Keto Waffles with Chocolate Cottage Cheese

Servings: 2   **Preparation time:** 30 minutes
Ingredients
- Cocoa - 1 tbsp
- KetoDiet Protein drink hazelnut flavor and chocolate - 1 tbsp
- KetoDiet Protein drink creamy without flavor - 2 measuring cups
- Baking powder - 1/4 teaspoon
- Almond flour - 30 g
- Butter - 40 g
- Milk - 120 ml
- Whole cottage cheese - 1 piece
- Cinnamon - 1/2 teaspoon
- Vanilla essence according to taste
- Egg - 2 pcs

Instructions. Prepare the dough for 6 waffles. In a bowl, mix almond flour, KetoDiet protein powder, baking powder, cinnamon, add eggs, milk, warmed butter, vanilla extract, and whip everything into a smooth dough. We can use a stick mixer. Pour the dough into a warm waffle maker and bake until pink. Meanwhile, whip the cottage cheese with cocoa and season with a spoonful protein drink hazelnut and chocolate. Finished waffles are served with whipped chocolate curd.

5. Cheese Keto Patties

Servings: 2   **Preparation time:** 30 minutes
Ingredients
- Basil according to taste
- Herbs according to taste
- Cheddar - 2 slices
- Cherry tomatoes - 5 pcs
- KetoDiet protein omelet with cheese flavor - 1 bag
- Cauliflower - 300 g
- Olive oil according to taste
- Parmesan - 50 g
- Salt according to taste

Instructions. Salt the grated cauliflower, let it stand and drain the excess water and squeeze through a cloth. Thoroughly mix one serving of KetoDiet protein omelet (in a shaker or whisk) in 100 ml of water, mix with cauliflower, herbs, and grated Parmesan cheese. From the dough, we make patties, which we fry in a pan until browned; we put a cheddar slice and let it melt. We serve vegetable salads with pancakes, for example from cherry tomatoes with basil dripped with olive oil.

6. Keto Porridge with Wild Berries

Servings: 1   **Preparation time:** 15 minutes
Ingredients
- chicory syrup according to taste
- KetoDiet raspberry porridge - 1 piece

- Coconut milk - 50 ml
- Forest fruit - 100 g
- Milk - 100 ml
- Almond slices - 1 tbsp
- Shredded coconut - 1 tbsp
- Cottage cheese - 1 tbsp

Instructions. Whip the protein raspberry porridge with the milk (cow and coconut) until smooth and put it in the microwave for a minute, or heat the milk in a saucepan and pour the contents of the bag into the hot milk and mix thoroughly. Stir 50 g of mixed forest fruit into the finished porridge, add coconut, a spoonful of cottage cheese and garnish with dry roasted almond slices and the remaining fruit.

7. Keto Potato Pancakes

Servings: 1   **Preparation time:** 20 minutes
Ingredients
- Balsamic - 1 teaspoon (for salad)
- Celery - 150 g
- Garlic - 1 clove
- Crushed cumin according to taste
- KetoDiet protein pancake with garlic flavor - 1 serving
- Marjoram according to taste
- Ground flax seeds - 1 tablespoon
- Oil according to taste
- Olive oil - 1 tablespoon (for salad)
- Pepper according to taste
- Radish - 3 pcs (for salad)
- A mixture of green salads (arugula, romaine lettuce, corn salad)1 handful (for salad)
- Salt according to taste
- Water - 100 ml

Instructions
Grate the celery and mix it with all the ingredients, including the protein pancake powder, to make a thinner dough. We make patties from the dough, which we fry until golden in a pan. Serve with a vegetable salad of mixed salad (we used corn on the cob, arugula, beet leaves), chopped radishes, which we cut. Mix everything and drizzle with the prepared dressing of olive oil and balsamic.

8. Baked Avocado

Servings: 2   **Preparation time:** 30 minutes
Ingredients
- Avocado - 2
- Cherry tomatoes to taste
- Pepper to taste
- Bacon - 4 slices
- Salt to taste
- Cottage cheese - 1
- Egg - 4 pieces

Instructions. Cut the avocado lengthwise and remove the stone. We dig out a little pulp with a spoon. Put the hollowed-out avocados in a small baking dish with baking paper. Tap 1 small egg in each half of the avocado and add a piece of bacon, cottage cheese, cherry tomatoes, etc. Add salt and pepper. Bake until the egg is ready.

9. Pasta Salad

Servings: 1   **Preparation time:** 20 minutes
Ingredients
- KetoDiet protein pasta Fusilli- 1 serving
- Olive oil - 2 tablespoons (for mayonnaise)
- Pepper according to taste
- Radish - 3 pcs
- Cucumber - 100 g
- A mixture of green salads (arugula, romaine lettuce, corn salad)1 handful
- Salt according to taste
- Sour cream - 1 tablespoon (for mayonnaise)
- Green pepper - 100 g

Instructions. Cut peppers, cucumber, and radish and mix them with salad and ready-made protein pasta, which we cooked according to the instructions. Pour the homemade mayonnaise over the salad, which we prepare from sour cream, olive oil, salt, and pepper. Garnish with chives or herbs and serve.
ATTENTION! If you have this mayonnaise in step 1 of your diet plan, omit half the amount (= 1 DCL) of milk allowed that day.

10. Baked Keto Peppers

Servings: 2   **Preparation time:** 60 minutes
Ingredients
- Balsamic - 1 teaspoon (for salad)
- White or green pepper - 2 pcs
- Garlic - 1 clove
- Cherry tomatoes - 5 pcs (for salad)
- Half onion
- KetoDiet protein omelet with cheese flavor - 1 piece
- Ground beef meat - 100 g
- Olive oil - 20 ml for peppers + to taste for salad
- Pepper according to taste
- Radish - 5 pcs (for salad)
- Rosemary according to taste
- A mixture of green salads (arugula, romaine lettuce, corn salad), a handful (for salad)
- Salt according to taste
- Water - 100 ml
- Mushrooms - 3 pcs

Instructions. We clean the pepper, cut it in half, and get rid of the kernels. Fry the sliced mushrooms with a sprig of rosemary in a hot pan and set them aside. Now fry the chopped onion in the same pan, add the minced meat, garlic and season with salt and pepper.

Once the meat is roasted, add the mushrooms to the mixture and mix. Fill the halved peppers with the meat mixture and pour them over the water with a mixed protein omelet— Bake in a baking dish at 150 ° C for about 20 minutes. Serve with a vegetable salad of 5 cherry tomatoes, 5 radishes, and a handful of mixed salad, which we drizzle with a dressing of 1 tablespoon olive oil, 1 teaspoon balsamic, salt and pepper.

11. Easter Lamb

Servings: 6   **Preparation time:** 0 minutes
Ingredients
- Chicory syrup - 1/4 cup
- 1/2 lemon juice
- KetoDiet Protein Drink - 1 serving
- Baking powder - 1 piece
- Almond flour - 1 and 1/4 cup
- Ground flax seeds - 1/2 cup
- Ground poppy seeds - 1/2 cup
- Greek white yogurt - 1 mug
- Egg - 4 pieces

Instructions. Mix Greek yogurt, add almond flour, 1 serving of protein drink, eggs, mixed flax seeds, poppy seeds, lemon juice, chicory syrup, and 1 baking powder. Mix everything well and pour into the erased form—Bake for about 40 minutes at 180 ° C.

12. Keto Tart with Wild Berries

Servings: 2   **Preparation:** 60 minutes
Ingredients
- Chicory syrup - 1 tablespoon
- KetoDiet protein panna cotta - 1 serving
- Forest fruit - 200 g
- Mascarpone - 100 g
- Mint for decoration
- Whole cottage cheese - 100 g
- Gelatin - 1 piece

Instructions. Mix mascarpone with cottage cheese and protein panna cotta mixture and sweeten with chicory syrup. Pour the finished cream into a bowl and place the forest fruits on top. Pour the prepared gelatin according to the instructions and let it cool in the refrigerator until the gelatin hardens. Decorate with a sprig of mint, for example.

Lunch

1. Keto Pasta Curry

Servings: 2   **Preparation time:** 30 minutes
Ingredients
- Fresh baby spinach a handful of petals
- Fresh coriander according to taste

- Garlic - 1 clove
- Zucchini - 100 g
- Curry spice according to taste
- KetoDiet protein cheese soup with vegetables - 1 bag
- KetoDiet protein pasta Fusilli - 1 bag
- Coconut milk - 50 ml
- Oil according to taste
- Shallot - 1
- Water - 170 ml

Instructions. Fry finely chopped onion, crushed garlic, chopped zucchini, and curry in oil and sauté until soft. Mix KetoDiet protein cheese soup in hot water, add to the mixture and cook for a while. Mix with Fusilli protein pasta cooked according to the instructions, spinach, pour coconut milk and sprinkle with coriander.

2. Vegetable-Mushroom Keto Omelette

Serving: 1 **Preparation time:** 20 minutes
Ingredients
- Fresh baby spinach, a handful of petals
- Zucchini -100 g
- Pumpkin - 100 g
- KetoDiet Protein omelet with bacon flavor - 1 serving
- Oil according to taste
- Parmesanfor sprinkling
- Pepper according to taste
- Salt according to taste
- Mushrooms - 50 g

Instructions. Cut zucchini, pumpkin, and mushrooms into pieces, fry in oil, salt, pepper, add spinach leaves. Mix the KetoDiet protein omelet in water, pour over the vegetables, sprinkle with cheese, and bake for 5-10 minutes at 180 ° C.

3. Avocado Foam

Serving: 1 **Preparation time:** 15 min
Ingredients
- Avocado - 1/2
- Cocoa - 2 tablespoons
- Coconut milk - 20 ml
- KetoDiet protein drink flavored with hazelnut and chocolate - 10 g
- Shredded coconut - 1 tbsp

Instructions. Dissolve one tablespoon (10 g) of flavored protein drink (vanilla or hazelnut flavor and chocolate) in coconut milk, add skinless and stone-free avocado, cocoa and mix into a smooth cream. Serve sprinkled with grated coconut.

4. Keto Specle with Spinach

Servings: 2 **Preparation:** 30 minutes
Ingredients

- Fresh baby spinach handful
- Garlic - 1 clove
- KetoDiet protein omelet with cheese flavor - 1 bag
- Baking powder - 1/2 teaspoon
- Olive oil according to taste
- Parmesan - 25 g
- Shallot - 1/2
- Whipping cream - 50 ml
- Salt according to taste
- Cottage cheese - 1 tbsp
- Egg - 1

Instructions. Beat eggs with cottage cheese, baking powder, and powder from a bag with KetoDiet omelet. Pour the resulting dough into a decorating bag and make speckles into boiling salted water—Cook for about 3 minutes. Pour the cooked specks and fry dry until golden in a hot pan. Place the finished speckles on a plate and fry the finely chopped onion, garlic in the pan and fry for a while. Return the speckle to the pan, mix, pour over the cream, mix in the baby spinach and finally sprinkle with grated Parmesan cheese.

5. Keto Mushrooms with Celery Fries

Servings: 1   **Preparation:** 40 minutes
Ingredients
- Herbs for decoration
- Celery - 200 g
- KetoDiet Protein omelet with bacon flavor - 1 serving
- Olive oil - 2 tbsp
- Pepper according to taste
- Salt according to taste
- Water - 100 ml
- Mushrooms - 3 pcs

Instructions. Clean the celery, cut it into thin fries, drizzle with olive oil, salt, pepper, and bake in the oven for about 15 minutes at 165 ° C. We watch the french fries in the oven because it depends on how strong we cut them. Meanwhile, cut the mushrooms into slices and mix them with the protein omelet mixed in water. The mushrooms wrapped "in batter" from an omelet are then sautéed until golden in oil. We can pour the rest of the omelet on the mushroom pan so that we don't miss a bit of protein. Serve with celery fries.

6. Turkey Roll with Spring Onion, Olives, and Sun-Dried tomatoes

Servings: 4   **Preparation time:** 80 minutes
Ingredients
- Balsamic to taste
- Black olives - 60 g
- Garlic - 20 g
- Cherry tomatoes - 280 g
- Spring onion - 120 g
- Turkey breast - 400 g
- Olive oil - 40 ml

- Pepper to taste
- Rocket - 120 g
- Salt to taste
- Dried tomatoes in oil - 60 g

Instructions. Carefully cut the turkey breast lengthwise so that a larger pancake is formed and tap the meat. Fry the finely chopped spring onion and garlic in a pan in olive oil. Add olives cut in half and sliced sun-dried tomatoes, and fry everything briefly. Apply the mixture to a slice of turkey meat and carefully roll it into a roll. Tie with thread and bake at 180 degrees for 50 minutes. Cut the finished roll into slices and serve with arugula salad and fresh cherry tomatoes flavored with olive oil and balsamic.

7. Zucchini Lasagna

Servings: 2   **Preparation time:** 60 minutes
Ingredients
- Basil as required
- Red wine - 1 glass
- Onion - 1
- Zucchini - 1
- Ground beef - 250 g
- Olive oil as required
- Pepper to taste
- Tomatoes - 1 can (without added sugar)
- Whipping cream - 1 piece
- Grated cheddar to taste
- Salt to taste
- Egg - 1 piece

Instructions. Fry the diced onion in olive oil, add the minced meat, salt, pepper, add basil and sauté. Once the meat has pulled, cover with red wine and stew. When the wine boils, add chopped tomatoes, cover, and simmer for about 30 minutes. Cut the zucchini lengthwise into thin slices. It works best with a potato peeler, but we can also playfully handle it with a knife. Wipe the baking dish with butter, layout the zucchini slices, pour the sauce over the minced meat, sprinkle with grated cheddar, and pour over the beaten egg in the cream. Layer another layer of zucchini, sauce, cheddar, and pour again with cream and egg. We repeat the whole thing, and we finish with a layer of cheddar and cream. Bake in a preheated oven at 200 degrees for about 30 minutes.

8. Keto Soup with Zucchini

Servings: 1   **Preparations:** 15 minutes
Ingredients
- Herbs according to taste
- Garlic - 1 clove
- Onion - 1/2 pcs
- Zucchini - 150 g
- KetoDiet protein cheese soup with vegetables - 1 piece
- Butter - 1 teaspoon
- Olive oil - 20 ml

- Pepper according to taste
- Water - 250 ml

Instructions. In a small saucepan, fry the zucchini chopped in olive oil, add salt, pepper, herbs, and garlic. Pour water and cook until soft. Finally, stir in the cheese protein soup, a teaspoon of butter, turn off the flame and let it run for 3 minutes. Garnish with herbs.

9. Pumpkin with Greek Feta Cheese

Servings: 2   **Preparation time:** 85 minutes
Ingredients
- Hokaido pumpkins - 1
- Olive oil as required
- Pepper to taste
- Sunflower seeds to taste
- Garlic cloves - 3
- Salt to taste
- Feta cheese - 100 g
- Thyme - 2 sprigs
- Walnuts as required

Instructions. Peel the pumpkin, remove the seeds, cut into larger cubes, and spread in a baking dish. We don't peel garlic, so let's avoid burning it. Bake the mixture for about 40 minutes at 180 degrees, then add the walnuts and sunflower seeds and bake gently for about 10 minutes. We do not add nuts sooner so that they do not burn. Take the baked goods out of the oven and sprinkle with grated feta cheese. To make the cheese beautifully baked, put it in the oven for another 5 minutes.

10. Keto Houstičky with Herb Butter

Serving: 3   **Preparation time:** 60 minutes
Ingredients
- White - 3 pcs
- Herbs to taste (for herb butter)
- Pumpkin seeds - 1 tbsp
- Hot water - 1/2 cup
- Apple vinegar - 2 teaspoons
- KetoDiet Protein Drink - 2 servings
- Baking powder - 2 teaspoons
- Gourmet yeast - 2 tablespoons
- Almond flour - 1 and 1/4 cup
- Butter - 4 tablespoons (for herb butter)
- Psyllium (fiber) - 5 tablespoons
- Sunflower or flax seeds - 1 tbsp
- Salt - 1 teaspoon
- Maldon saltfor sprinkling
- Yolk - 1 piece

Instructions. Mix the ingredients, including the protein powder, and add hot water while whipping constantly. Add a pinch of salt, stir again.

We shape 6 buns from the dough and place on a baking sheet. We leave gaps between them, because the pastry will increase in volume during baking. Brush the buns with egg yolk and bake for about 30 minutes at 160 ° C. Let the finished buns cool down and serve them with herb butter, for example, which we prepare by mixing herbs according to your taste into the softened butter and letting them harden to any shape in the fridge. We used parsley, basil, and thyme.

11. Baked Keto Fennel

Servings: 2   **Preparation time:** 70 minutes
Ingredients
- Fresh fennel - 2 bulbs
- Pumpkin seeds - 2 tablespoons
- KetoDiet protein omelet with cheese flavor - 1 serving
- Olive oil - 1 tablespoon
- Chive according to taste
- Pepper according to taste
- Parsley according to taste
- Sunflower seeds - 2 tablespoons
- Whipping cream - 150 ml
- Salt according to taste
- Hard cheese - 50 g

Instructions. Wash and cut the fennel into slices, which we place in a baking dish. Season with salt, pepper, herbs, and mix with olive oil. Pour in a protein omelet mixed in cream, cover with grated cheese and bake at 165 ° C for about 50 minutes. Meanwhile, fry the pumpkin and sunflower seeds dry in a pan and sprinkle them on the finished meal. Garnish with, for example, the remaining herbs or sprigs of fennel.

12. Wholemeal Couscous with Cherry Tomatoes

Serving: 1   **Preparation time:** 20 minutes
Ingredients
- Wholegrain couscous - 50 g
- Fresh basil handful
- Garlic - 1 clove
- Cherry tomatoes - 5 pcs
- Half Zucchini
- KetoDiet chicken/beef protein soup (depends on your taste)1 bag
- Olive oil - 1 tbsp
- Parmesan - 30 g
- Sunflower seeds - 2 spoons for pesto + 1 spoon for decoration
- Water - 100 ml

Instructions. Prepare the protein soup in 100 ml of water and let it stand for 3 minutes. Pour the finished soup over the dry couscous and let stand for another 5 minutes to soak up the couscous. Meanwhile, cut the zucchini into rounds, fry it dry on both sides in a pan, add olive oil, tomatoes, and garlic and fry the mixture. Add the finished couscous, a spoonful of pesto, and mix. Garnish with fresh basil, a little pesto, and roasted sunflower seeds and serve. How to make homemade basil pesto?

Very simple! We mix a handful of basil, 2 tablespoons of sunflower seeds, 2 tablespoons of olive oil, and 2 tablespoons of grated Parmesan cheese and decorate the finished couscous with it.

Dinner

1. Keto Pasta with Zucchini

Servings: 1   **Preparation time:** 20 minutes
Ingredients
- Fresh parsley according to taste
- Garlic - 1 clove
- Zucchini - 120 g
- Pumpkin seeds - 1 tbsp
- KetoDiet protein pasta Fusilli - 1 piece
- Olive oil - 1 tbsp
- Salt according to taste
- The egg white - 1 piece

Instructions. Cut the zucchini into pieces. Fry the pumpkin seeds dry in a pan. Pour the seeds into a bowl and fry finely chopped or pressed garlic in oil and add the zucchini. Once the zucchini softens, add the cooked protein pasta according to the instructions and pour over the protein. Salt and mix until the pasta is slightly combined with the zucchini and the egg whites. Finally, sprinkle with fried pumpkin seeds and garnish with parsley.

2. Keto Pizza

Servings: 1 serving   **Preparation time:** 60 minutes
Ingredients
- Broccoli - 250 g
- Fresh baby spinach handful (for lining)
- Garlic - 1 clove (for lining)
- KetoDiet Protein Drink - 1 scoop (15 g)
- Oregano to taste (for dough and lining)
- Parmesan - 10 g
- Parmesan for sprinkling
- Pepper according to taste
- Tomatoes - 2 pcs (for lining)
- Egg - 1 piece
- Mushrooms - 2 pcs (for lining)

Instructions. We break down the broccoli into roses, which we mix in a small mixer. Spread the broccoli on a baking sheet lined and bake for 10 minutes in an oven preheated to 180 ° C. Mix baked broccoli with egg, protein drink, and grated parmesan, salt, and pepper. Make a pancake from the dough, spread a mixture of mixed tomatoes, garlic, and oregano on it. Put with sliced mushrooms and lightly sprinkle with grated Parmesan cheese. Bake the pizza at 180 ° C for about 15 minutes. Garnish with baby spinach before serving.

3. Baked Portobello Mushrooms

Servings: 4   **Preparation time:** 30 minutes
Ingredients
- Red onion - 1
- Garlic according to taste
- Cherry tomatoes - 4
- Goat cheese - 150 g
- Ground beef - 250 g
- Pepper according to taste
- Vegetable oil according to need
- Salt according to taste
- Thyme according to taste
- Portobello mushroom - 4

Instructions. We clean the heads of mushrooms, remove the foot and hollow out the inside, cut the foot into smaller pieces. Heat oil in a pan and add minced meat, thyme, crushed garlic, salt, pepper, and sauté for a while. Add the inside of the mushroom and a sliced leg to the meat. Fill the finished mixture with mushroom caps, place the sliced red onion, sliced cherry tomatoes on the wheels, and sprinkle with grated cheese.
Bake for 25 minutes in an oven heated to 180 ° C. Mushrooms are served with fresh vegetable salad.

4. Baked Protein Omelette

Serving: 1   **Preparation time:** 30 minutes
Ingredients
- Cherry tomatoes - 2
- Zucchini - 50 g
- KetoDiet cheese omelette - 1
- Chard - 20 g
- Pepper according to taste
- Vegetable oil according to need
- Salt according to taste
- Hard cheese (up to 30% fat in dry matter) - 50 g
- Mushrooms - 50 g

Instructions. Cut the zucchini into pieces, slice the mushrooms, salt, pepper and fry together for a while in hot oil; add the sliced chard leaf, mix and put in a baking dish. In the shaker, mix the protein omelet according to the instructions and pour on the mixture. Add chopped cherry tomatoes and sprinkle with grated cheese—Bake for about 25 minutes at 180 ° C.

5. Zucchini Pie

Servings: 4   **Preparation time:** 60 minutes
Ingredients
- Basil to taste
- Zucchini - 1
- Mozzarella - 1

- Pepper to taste
- Salt to taste
- Egg - 3

Instructions. In a bowl, mix 1 larger mozzarella with 3 eggs. Grate the zucchini, mix everything, salt, and pepper. Pour into a baking dish. Garnish the slices of tomato on top, we can also add fresh basil leaves. Bake at a temperature of 180 degrees for about 30-40 minutes.

6. Salad with Olives and Cottage Cheese

Serving: 1   **Preparation time:** 15 minutes
Ingredients
- Black olives as required
- Cucumber salad - 1/2
- Pepper - 1
- Pepper to taste
- Tomatoes - 2
- Salt to taste
- Cottage cheese - 1

Instructions. Cut the vegetables into cubes, add the black olives to taste, salt, pepper, and mix with 1 cup of cottage cheese. Sprinkle with finely chopped chives on top.

7. Vegetable Salad with Goat Cheese

Servings: 2   **Preparation time:** 30 minutes
Ingredients
- Balsamic - 1 tablespoon
- Cherry tomatoes as required
- Goat cheese - 2 slices
- Olive oil - 2 tablespoons + for dripping
- Seed mixture (sunflower, pumpkin) - 1 package
- A mixture of green salads (arugula, romaine lettuce, corn salad) - 1 package

Instructions. Cut goat cheese into thicker slices and grill or fry dry in a non-stick pan. Mix popular types of green salads with cherry tomatoes and season with a mixture of olive oil and balsamic. We can taste it with a pinch of salt and, depending on the taste, also pepper. Place the roasted goat cheese slices on a salad, sprinkle with a mixture of seeds and drizzle with olive oil.

Desserts

1. Keto Panna Cotta with Wild Berries

Servings: 1   **Preparation time:** 80 minutes
Ingredients
- Forest fruit - 100 g
- Milk - 100 ml
- Protein panna cotta with cream and vanilla flavor - 1 bag

Instructions. According to the instructions, mix the protein panna cotta in milk, pour it into a mold, and let it solidify in the refrigerator. Pour the finished panna cotta onto a plate and garnish with mixed forest fruits and a sprig of mint.

2. Sweet Potato-Pumpkin Christmas Salad

Servings: 4   **Preparation time:** 60 minutes
Ingredients
- Sweet potatoes - 2 pieces
- Chili spice pinch if you like spicy dishes
- Spring onion one volume
- Gherkin, according to taste
- A smaller butter pumpkin or a smaller Hokaido pumpkin1 piece
- Pepper according to taste
- Whole mustard - 3 tbsp
- Salt according to taste
- Egg - 4 pieces

Instructions. Cut the pumpkin, carve it out and cut into the same smaller cubes. We also peel and dice sweet potatoes into cubes (we select larger pieces). We cook everything in salted water for about 10 minutes. Drain the water and let it cool completely. Meanwhile, we boil the eggs hard, peel them, and cut them into cubes. We also finely chop pickles and spring onions. We definitely do not miss it; it will give the salad a great taste. Mix everything, salt, pepper, season with mustard, and mayonnaise. The salad will be better if we let it cool down and rest a little.

3. Unbaked Cheesecake in a glass

Servings: 8   **Preparation time:** 20 minutes
Ingredients
- chicory syrup to taste
- Mascarpone - 1
- Blackberries for decoration
- Whipped cream - 1 (whipped)
- Philadelphia cheese - 1 package

Instructions. Carefully mix the cheese and whipped cream with chicory syrup and pour into the prepared glasses. Garnish with blueberries or strawberries. Let cool in the fridge for at least an hour.

4. Chocolate Muesli Balls with Nuts

Servings: 15   **Preparation:** 30 minutes
Ingredients
- 70% dark chocolate - 25 g
- Fine muesli KetoLife - 150 g
- Hazelnuts - 30 g
- Butter - 70 g
- Protein cream with hazelnuts - 100 g

Instructions. From fine muesli, protein cream with hazelnuts (we use either 2 smaller packages of cream or 5 tablespoons from a large package), and melted butter, we create a dough from which we form balls. Put 1 hazelnut in each and wrap in melted 70% chocolate and chopped hazelnuts. We store the balls in the refrigerator.

5. Sweet Potato Muffins

Servings: 3   **Preparation time:** 50 minutes
Ingredients
- Sweet potatoes - 250 g
- Blueberries handful
- Chicory syrup to taste
- KetoDiet protein mixture - 2 measuring cups
- Baking powder - 1 bag
- Almond flour - 25 g
- Cinnamon - 1 tbsp
- Egg - 4
- Walnuts - 2 tablespoons (ground)

Instructions. Thoroughly mix the grated muffins with other ingredients, or mix and pour into molds (6 pcs). Bake at 180 degrees for 15-20 minutes until golden brown.

6. Walnut-Chocolate Balls

Servings: 12   **Preparation time:** 30 minutes
Ingredients
- Chicory syrup according to taste
- Hot chocolate - 100 g
- Cocoa for wrapping
- Coconut for wrapping
- Butter according to need
- Rum aroma according to taste
- Cinnamon for wrapping
- Walnuts - 250 g

Instructions. For 50 balls. Grind the nuts, mix with melted chocolate, butter, rum aroma, syrup. We make balls from the dough, which we wrap in cinnamon, cocoa, or coconut.

7. Chocolate Laundries

Servings: 5   **Preparation time:** 45 minutes
Ingredients
- Birch sugar xylitol - 3 tablespoons
- Cocoa - 3 tablespoons
- Baking powder - 1 teaspoon
- Almond flour - 70 g
- Butter - 35 g
- Dried whey - 20 g
- Egg yolk - 2

Instructions. We mix all the ingredients and work out the dough with our hands, which we press into the laundries' molds—Bake in the oven at 180 ° C for about 8 minutes.

8. Coconuts in Chocolate

Servings: 12   **Preparation time:** 45 minutes
Ingredients
- Hot chocolate according to need
- Whole cottage cheese8 tablespoons
- Shredded coconut - 200 g
- The egg white - 4

Instructions. We whip the snow from the proteins. Mix the ingredients in a bowl and use a spoon to form balls, which we bake on baking paper at a temperature of 160 ° C until golden. Soak in melted chocolate.

9. Linen Wheels

Servings: 6   **Preparation time:** 45 minutes
Ingredients
- Chicory syrup - 3 tablespoons
- Baking powder - 1 teaspoon
- Almond flour - 70 g
- Butter - 35 g
- Dried whey - 20 g
- Egg yolk - 2 pcs

Instructions. From these ingredients, we make a dough, which we leave to rest in the fridge for several hours. Then roll out on a thin pancake and cut out the wheels or hearts as you wish. Bake on baking paper at 170 ° C for about 10 minutes. After cooling, combine with jam or chocolate cream without sugar.

10. Almond Balls

Servings: 4   **Preparation time:** 50 minutes
Ingredients
- Cocoa - 2 tablespoons
- KetoDiet Protein Drink - 2 tablespoons
- Almond flour - 3 tablespoons
- Almond butter - 3 tablespoons
- Shredded coconut - 2 tablespoons

Instructions. Mix almond butter, ground nuts, grated coconut, cocoa powder, and a chocolate-flavored protein drink and work everything into the dough. Divide into 12 equal parts, from which we form balls. We then wrap the individual balls in coconut and cocoa powder.

CHAPTER 5

28-Day Meal Plan

Week 1

Day One. <u>Breakfast:</u> Chorizo Breakfast Bake. <u>Lunch:</u> Sesame Pork Lettuce Wraps. <u>Dinner:</u> Avocado Lime Salmon

Day Two. <u>Breakfast:</u> Keto Potato Pancakes. <u>Lunch:</u> Keto Pasta Curry. <u>Dinner:</u> Leftover Avocado Lime Salmon

Day Three. <u>Breakfast:</u> Baked Eggs in Avocado. <u>Lunch:</u> Easy Beef Curry. <u>Dinner:</u> Veggies and Rosemary Roasted Chicken

Day Four. <u>Breakfast:</u> Lemon Poppy Ricotta Pancakes with 3 Slices Thick-Cut Bacon. <u>Lunch:</u> Zucchini lasagna. <u>Dinner:</u> Leftover Rosemary Roasted Chicken and Veggies

Day Five. <u>Breakfast:</u> Leftover Lemon Poppy Ricotta Pancakes with 3 Slices Thick-Cut Bacon. <u>Lunch:</u> Keto Pasta Curry. <u>Dinner:</u> Cheesy Sausage Mushroom Skillet with 1 Slice Thick-Cut Bacon

Day Six. <u>Breakfast:</u> Sweet Blueberry Coconut Porridge with 1 Slice Thick-Cut Bacon. <u>Lunch:</u> Avocado foam. <u>Dinner:</u> Baked portobello mushrooms

Day Seven. <u>Breakfast:</u> Leftover Sweet Blueberry Coconut Porridge. <u>Lunch:</u> Keto soup with zucchini. <u>Dinner:</u> Keto Pasta with Zucchini

Week 2

Day One. <u>Breakfast:</u> Banana Keto Chia Pudding. <u>Lunch:</u> Easy Cheeseburger Salad. <u>Dinner:</u> Chicken Zoodle Alfredo

Day Two. <u>Breakfast:</u> Savory Ham and Cheese Waffles with 2 Slices Thick-Cut Bacon. <u>Lunch:</u> Keto Pasta Curry. <u>Dinner:</u> Cabbage and Sausage Skillet

Day Three. <u>Breakfast:</u> Keto Potato Pancakes. <u>Lunch:</u> Pumpkin with Greek feta cheese. <u>Dinner:</u> Baked portobello mushrooms

Day Four. <u>Breakfast:</u> Keto Waffles with Chocolate Cottage Cheese. <u>Lunch:</u> Avocado foam. <u>Dinner:</u> Zucchini pie

Day Five. <u>Breakfast:</u> Keto Potato Pancakes. <u>Lunch:</u> Sausage Skillet and Cabbage. <u>Dinner:</u> Keto Pasta with Zucchini

Day Six. <u>Breakfast:</u> Matcha Keto Pudding. <u>Lunch:</u> Vegetable-mushroom Keto Omelette. <u>Dinner:</u> Zucchini pie

Day Seven. Breakfast: Keto Tart with wild berries. Lunch: Pumpkin with Greek feta cheese. Dinner: Salad with olives and Cottage cheese

Week 3

Day One. Breakfast: Green Keto Smoothie. Lunch: Mozzarella Tuna Melt. Dinner: Cheesy Single-Serve Lasagna

Day Two. Breakfast: Bacon Breakfast Bombs. Lunch: Avocado, Salami Sandwiches, and Egg. Dinner: Crispy Chipotle Chicken Thighs

Day Three. Breakfast: Keto Waffles with Chocolate Cottage Cheese. Lunch: Keto Pasta Curry. Dinner: Ham, Pepperoni, and Cheese Stromboli

Day Four. Breakfast: Matcha Keto Pudding. Lunch: Avocado foam. Dinner: Cheese Stromboli, Leftover Pepperoni and Ham

Day Five. Breakfast: Keto Tart with wild berries. Lunch: Keto Pasta Curry. Dinner: Keto Pasta with Zucchini

Day Six. Breakfast: Three-Cheese Pizza Frittata with 2 Slices Thick-Cut Bacon. Lunch: Keto Pasta Curry. Dinner: Spring Salad with Steak and Sweet Dressing

Day Seven. Breakfast: Leftover Three-Cheese Pizza Frittata with 2 Slices Thick-Cut Bacon. Lunch: Vegetable-mushroom Keto Omelette. Dinner: Keto Pasta with Zucchini

Week 4

Day One. Breakfast: Keto Tart with wild berries. Lunch: Zucchini Pasta Salad and Chicken . Dinner: *Carb Up* Flank Steak, Watermelon Salad, and Plantains. Snacks: Mojito Water

Day Two. Breakfast: Keto Tart with wild berries. Lunch: Keto Mushrooms with celery fries. Dinner: Chicken and Bacon with Slaw. Snacks: Tropical Coconut Balls

Day Three. Breakfast: Baked Keto Peppers. Lunch: Sardine Salad. Dinner: Chorizo Bowl. Snacks: Jicama Fries

Day Four. Breakfast: Rocket Fuel Latte with Maca. Lunch: Zucchini Pasta Salad and Chicken. Dinner: Keto Pasta with Zucchini. Snacks: Mojito Water

Day Five. Breakfast: Pasta Salad. Lunch: Vanilla Creme Gummies. Dinner: Salad with olives and Cottage cheese. Snacks: Jicama Fries

Day Six. Breakfast: Veggie Frittata. Lunch: Sardine Salad. Dinner: Chicken and Bacon with Slaw. Snacks: Tropical Coconut Balls

Day Seven. Breakfast: Baked Keto Peppers. Lunch: Chicken and Zucchini Pasta Salad. Dinner: Keto Pasta with Zucchini. Snacks: Mojito Water

CONCLUSION

The ketogenic diet can offer benefits to women during menopause, including increased sensitivity to insulin, decreased weight gain, and decreased cravings.

It can, however, increase some cardiovascular disease risk factors and reduce the intake of many essential nutrients. What's more, during your body's transition to ketosis, keto flu can temporarily exacerbate the symptoms of menopause.

While the ketogenic diet can work during menopause for some women, bear in mind that it is not a one-size-fits-all solution for everyone.

It's a wise idea to consider other less restrictive ways to improve your health and meet your fitness goals before trying out the keto diet.

ANTI-INFLAMMATORY DIET COOKBOOK FOR BEGINNERS

Introduction

Inflammation is a medical term that describes an increase in size in a specific region of the body. Typically, a painful, crimson, and hot sensation may be felt in the region that is inflamed. It is possible for it to manifest in any portion of the body when an illness or damage is present. The symptoms that were stated before are typical, with inflammation that lasts just a brief time. Inflammation that lasts for an extended period of time, also known as chronic irritation, is the form of inflammation that is responsible for the development of illness. The inflammatory response is among the defense mechanisms that your body uses to keep itself healthy. In addition to that, it helps the body fight against diseases. Inflammation is generally considered to be beneficial since it plays a significant role in the amazing healing process that occurs inside the body. There is also a subset of the population that suffers from a form of the medical disease that prevents their immune systems from operating as well as they should. This illness may result in irritation of a low level or for a short period of time, but it also has the potential to cause inflammation that lasts for a prolonged period of time or is chronic. Infections and other disorders may also lead to a condition known as chronic inflammation, which can affect almost any part of the body. It is possible to have this symptom if you suffer from psoriasis, asthma, rheumatoid arthritis, or any of a number of other illnesses. According to the findings of several studies, persistent inflammation may possibly have a role in the development of cancer. In addition to these disorders, there is growing evidence in the medical literature that the foods we eat may also have a role in the development of continuous inflammation. That being said, modifying your eating routine in any way will be of great assistance to you in the event that you are afflicted with inflammation of any kind.

Symptoms of an inflammatory response. The following is a list of some of the indicators that you may be experiencing irritation in any part of your body:

- Bloating around the abdomen
- Achy joints
- Loss of appetite
- Acid reflux
- Nausea
- Diarrhea
- Gas
- Cramping

If you encounter any of these signs, then you need to make an appointment with your primary care physician as soon as possible. They will be able to assist you in determining whether or not you are indeed suffering from irritation or if the signs you are feeling are those of another ailment. The great news is that just by making simple adjustments to your diet, you may gradually bring down inflammation levels in your body in a natural way. It is the method that emphasizes moderate but consistent progress toward better health over the long term. You are able to do this by following a diet that reduces inflammation.

CHAPTER 1: What exactly is meant by the term "anti-inflammatory diet"?

Actually, there is no such thing as a diet that is guaranteed to reduce inflammation for any particular health condition, arthritis included, of course. There is more than one kind of diet designed to reduce inflammation. Diets such as the Dietary Pattern and the diet recommended by Dr. Weil are both examples of diets that can reduce inflammation. These dietary plans emphasize the consumption of foods that either contribute to irritation in the body or work to alleviate it. Diets designed to lower inflammation will naturally include products and foods known for their anti-inflammatory properties. In addition to this, it forbids the eating of items that promote inflammation. Antioxidants may be found in abundance in a wide variety of plant-based meals. Antioxidants, according to the findings of multiple research, may neutralize the effects of free agents in the body. When free radicals gather in large enough numbers, they may cause harm to the cells of the body. Because of this, any diet designed to reduce inflammation includes a substantial amount of food high in antioxidants. These kinds of diets have as their primary objective the internal cleaning and maintenance of the body as a whole. Your immune system will mend, and your digestion will become better if you follow this diet.

Different kinds of anti-inflammatory foods to eat. There are many well-known dietary treatments available today that can reduce inflammation. Diets such as the Mediterranean Diet, DASH Diet, and the Anti-Inflammatory Diet developed by Dr. Weil are all examples of diets that help reduce inflammation. In the subsequent chapters, we will discuss these various dietary plans.

Foods that are known to trigger inflammation. Inflammation might be caused by both the ways in which we eat and the items that we consume. You may get a head start on your journey toward an anti-inflammatory diet by avoiding foods that cause inflammation. This is just one of the methods by that you can get started.

These foods may be classified into one of the following six categories:

- Vegetable Oils (Includes Seed Oils)
- High Fructose and Sugary Foods
- Excess Alcohol
- Artificial Trans Fats
- Refined Carbs
- Processed Meat

Vegetable Oils (Includes Seed Oils). A significant amount of omega-6 oils may be found in these oils. In spite of the fact that they are required by the body, they are responsible for an increase in irritation if there is a greater proportion of omega-six to omega-three inside the body. During the 20th century, people consumed around 130% more vegetable oils than they did in the previous century on average. According to the opinions of several experts, it is one of the factors that contributes to the rising incidence of inflammatory-related health disorders. According to the findings of these studies, excessive use of these oils might lead to inflammation.

It is important to keep in mind that vegetable oils may be utilized in cooking and can also be found as an ingredient in a variety of processed meals. You should cut down on your consumption of vegetable oils to either forestall the development of irritation in the body or bring about a reduction in its severity.

High Fructose and Sugary Foods. Foods that are high in glucose and foods that have a significant amount of fructose should be at the top of your list of foods to steer clear of. There are two primary offenders in the food that we follow on a daily basis that is responsible for inflammation. In the first place, we have high fructose corn syrup, and in the second place, we have regular sugar. These seem to be the two most frequent kinds of sugar that are consumed in today's diets all across the world. According to the findings of one research, the body sustains a significant amount of harm as a direct result of the consumption of these added sugars. However, fructose and all of the other forms of sugars that you discover naturally occurring in all of our meals are not inherently harmful or sinful in and of themselves. They are genuinely beneficial since they provide the body with the much-required energy. The problem is when you take in too much information, which may happen very rapidly. Simply consuming a huge can of Coke would provide you with the same amount of glucose that your body requires for the whole of one week in a single session. However, do you just drink a single can of soda at a time? There are some folks who consume at least three sodas every day. A diet that is heavy in sugar may increase the risk of developing breast cancer, according to the findings of another research. Sugar may also be found in the form of sucrose. In addition, there is evidence to indicate that consuming meals high in sugar may inhibit or counteract the anti-inflammatory benefits of omega-three fatty acids. Excessive consumption of fructose has been associated with an increased risk of developing chronic illnesses such as cancer, diabetes, fatty liver disease, insulin resistance, chronic kidney disease, and obesity.

Excess Alcohol. One may make the case that drinking alcohol in moderation does, in fact, have some positive health effects. This indicates that having a few drinks every once in a while isn't really going to hurt you all that much. On the other hand, consuming much more wine than is typical might lead to major health issues, including irritation. A disease known as irritable bowel syndrome may develop in those who have a problem with excessive drinking. This illness is characterized by the propensity of the body to store bacterial toxins. This illness has the potential to cause harm to several organs as well as extensive inflammation.

Artificial Trans Fats. Artificial Trans fats are without a doubt the unhealthiest fats that can be found anywhere on the earth. These are meals that include components that have been partially hydrogenated. This indicates that hydrogen is included in the production of unsaturated lipids. The majority of unsaturated fats exist in a liquid state. The addition of hydrogen causes them to become much more solid, which in turn increases their stability. Additionally, the quantity of HDL cholesterol in the body is decreased when artificial Tran's fats are consumed. Studies have shown that these substances also damage the endothelial cells that line our arteries, which raises the probability that we may develop heart disease. Some varieties of pastries, cookies, and pre-packaged cakes, as well as margarine, vegetable shortening, French fries, microwave popcorn, and other kinds of fast food, are typically prepared with artificial Tran's fats.

Other foods that are typically prepared with artificial Trans fatty acids include microwave popcorn, French fries, and other kinds of fast food.

Refined Carbs. It's not true that all carbohydrates are the same. There are some that are enjoyable to consume, and there are others that might be beneficial to have in your diet. To clarify, I'm talking to refined carbs when I say that the ones that are great to have but aren't really required. Take note that not all forms of carbohydrates pose a health risk. You have to understand that people have been eating carbohydrates ever since prehistoric times. It is a truth that our predecessors consumed unprocessed carbohydrates, which meant that their diets had a significant amount of fiber, which is beneficial to the body. On the other hand, during the process of refining, the fiber and all of the other important nutrients are removed. The refined carbs are all that are still available to us. According to the study, even though they have a much longer shelf life, they may cause a significant amount of inflammation in the body. Keep in mind that fiber helps regulate blood sugar levels and that it generally makes you feel fuller for longer. When you have recently had a diet that was rich in fiber, you will not have a need for more food for this reason. Additionally, fiber nourishes the beneficial bacteria that are already present in your digestive tract, which contributes to the preservation of your general health.

Processed Meat. Beef jerky, ham, smoked meat, sausages, and bacon are all examples of processed cuts of meat. They have a wonderful flavor, and as a result, many people made them regulars at the dinner table. However, research suggests that consuming these foods may raise the risk of a number of other ailments, including stomach cancer, colon cancer, heart disease, and diabetes. Intake of processed meat is linked to the development of colon cancer more often than any other disease. Researchers believe that this could be because these meats have a high concentration of extended glycation end, also known as AGEs. AGEs are produced when high heat is applied to meat after it has been mixed with other ingredients and then subjected to the mixture. Research backs up the theory that AGEs are to blame for inflammation throughout the body. Take into consideration the fact that the growth of colon cancer is influenced by a wide variety of variables. However, studies suggest that the intake of meat and the irritation that comes along with it is probably the single most important cause in the development of the disease.

CHAPTER 2: Anti-inflammatory Breakfast Recipes

2.1 Chia Seed and Milk Pudding
Preparation time: 5 Minutes **Cooking time:** 0 Minutes **Serving:** 6 Persons

Ingredients

- 1 cup mixed berries (fresh, for garnishing)
- 4 cups coconut milk (full-fat)
- 3/4 cup coconut yogurt (for topping)
- 1/4 cup coconut chips (toasted for garnishing)
- 1/2 teaspoon cinnamon (ground)
- 1/2 cup chia seeds
- 3 tablespoons honey
- 1 teaspoon vanilla extract
- 1 teaspoon turmeric (ground)
- 1/2 teaspoon ginger (ground)

Instructions. Combine the ginger, turmeric, and cinnamon in a mixing bowl along with the honey, vanilla essence, and coconut milk. Combine them well and continue to do so until the mixture takes on a yellowish hue. Add the chia seeds to the mixture and stir them around. Combine them thoroughly. For around five minutes, you should refrain from stirring the mixture. After the first 5 minutes have passed, give the mixture another stir. Cover the ingredients together. Place it in the refrigerator, where it will stay for at least 6 hours, preferably overnight. The pudding-like consistency will be achieved as a result of the chia seeds expanding and becoming plumper. Distribute the pudding among the four glasses. Put some coconut yogurt, coconut chips, and a combination of berries on top of each glass of pudding. Serve.

Nutrition Calories: 200 Kcal, Proteins: 12g, Fat: 8g, Carbohydrates: 21g

2.2 Scrambled Eggs with Turmeric
Preparation time: 6 Minutes **Cooking time:** 0 Minutes **Serving:** 1 Person

Ingredients

- 2 radishes (grated)
- 2 kale leaves (shredded)
- 2 eggs (pastured)
- 1 tablespoon turmeric
- 2 tablespoons coconut oil
- 1 small clove of garlic (minced)
- clover and radish sprouts (for topping)

- 1 pinch of cayenne pepper

Instructions. Put some coconut oil in a pan and keep the temperature at medium. Cook the garlic in the skillet. The eggs should be broken up into the pan. Make the eggs into scrambled form by stirring them while they are cooking. Add the kale, cayenne pepper, and turmeric to the scrambled eggs just before they are completely cooked through. Stir. Place on a plate after the transfer. Radishes that have been grated and sprouts should be used as a topping. Serve.

Nutrition Calories: 401 Kcal, Proteins: 25g, Fat: 19g, Carbohydrates: 31g

2.3 Protein-Rich Turmeric Donuts
Preparation time: 5 Minutes **Cooking time:** 10 Minutes **Serving:** 1 Person

Ingredients

- 1 1/2 cups cashews (raw)
- 7 Medjool dates (pitted)
- 1/4 cup coconut (shredded)
- 1 tablespoon vanilla protein powder
- 1/4 cup dark chocolate (for topping)
- 2 teaspoons maple syrup
- 1/4 teaspoon vanilla essence
- 1 teaspoon turmeric powder

Instructions. Put all of the ingredients, with the exception of the dark chocolate, into a food processor and pulse until smooth. Blend on the highest speed until the mixture forms a dough that is silky smooth and sticky. Form the dough into a total of eight balls. Donuts should be made by pressing each ball tightly into a mold. Wrap the mold with a cover. Donuts will need to be chilled in the refrigerator for around half an hour. Put one cup of water into a pot and set it to cook over medium heat. Start the water boiling in a pot. Put the dark chocolate in a smaller pot and start heating it up. Put the smaller pan on the upper edge of the larger one that contains the water that is boiling. Chocolate should be stirred until it is completely melted. Remove the doughnuts from the freezer and place them on a plate. Use the melted chocolate to create a glaze for the doughnuts. Serve.

Nutrition Calories: 323 Kcal, Proteins: 29g, Fat: 17g, Carbohydrates: 35g

2.4 Cranberry and Sweet Potato Bars
Preparation time: 6 Minutes **Cooking time:** 10 Minutes **Serving:** 1 Person

Ingredients

- 1 cup almond meal
- 1 1/2 cups sweet potato purée
- 1 cup cranberries (fresh)
- 1/3 cup coconut flour

- 1/4 cup water
- 2 eggs
- 2 tablespoons coconut oil (melted)
- 2 tablespoons maple syrup
- 1 1/2 teaspoon baking soda

Instructions. Turn the oven on to 350 degrees F. and prepare the oven. Put the maple syrup, sweet potato puree, water, melted coconut oil, and eggs in a large bowl and mix well. Blend them together well. Sift the almond meal, coconut flour, and baking soda together in a separate mixing bowl. Combine the ingredients well. Combine the two dry ingredients and add them to the liquid. Make sure the batter is well combined. Prepare a 9-inch square baking dish by greasing it. Wrap parchment paper around the inside as well. The batter should be spread out on the prepared pan. Apply a thin layer of batter to the pan and spread it out evenly with a damp spatula. Put one berry at a time on top of a batter and press down gently. Put it in the oven and bake for 35 minutes, checking it halfway through. When it's totally cold, cut it into 16 pieces.

Nutrition Calories: 130 Kcal, Proteins: 10g, Fat: 5g, Carbohydrates: 11g

2.5 Nutty Choco-Nana Pancakes

Preparation time: 5 Minutes **Cooking time:** 0 Minutes **Serving:** 2 Persons

Ingredients

Pancakes:

- 2 eggs (large)
- 2 bananas (ripe)
- 2 tablespoons creamy almond butter
- 1/8 teaspoon salt
- 2 tablespoons cacao powder (raw)
- Coconut oil (for greasing)
- 1 teaspoon pure vanilla extract
    - **Sauce:**
- 1/4 cup coconut oil
- 4 tablespoons cacao powder (raw)

Instructions. Pancakes: Get a pan ready on low heat. Grease the pan with 1 tablespoon of coconut oil. Put everything you need to make pancakes into a food processor. Mix all of the ingredients together and pulse them on high until the batter is completely smooth. To create one pancake, pour approximately a quarter cup of the mixture onto the hot skillet. Flip each pancake after 5 minutes of cooking. Turn the pancake over very gently. For a further 2 minutes, flip the meat. Repeat this process until no more batter is available. Sauce may be served alongside or on the pancakes. **Sauce:** Warm the coconut oil in a pan over medium heat.

Add the cacao powder to the oil and stir until combined. Get out of the sun. Leave aside.

Nutrition Calories: 621 Kcal, Proteins: 22.4g, Fat: 32g, Carbohydrates: 66g

2.6 Blueberry Avocado Chocolate Muffins
Preparation time: 15 Minutes **Cooking time:** 0 Minutes **Serving:** 2 Persons

Ingredients

- 1/2 cup almond milk (unsweetened)
- 1 cup almond flour
- 1/3 cup coconut sugar
- 1/4 cup cacao powder + 1 tablespoon (raw)
- 1/4 cup blueberries (fresh)
- 2 large eggs (room temperature)
- 1 small avocado (ripe)
- 1/4 teaspoon salt
- 2 tablespoons coconut flour
- 2 teaspoons baking powder
- 2 tablespoons dark chocolate chips

Instructions. Bake at 375 degrees Fahrenheit, which requires preheating the oven. Put paper muffin cups in a muffin tray. Put the eggs, salt, avocados, sugar, and 1 tbsp of the cacao powder in a blender and mix until smooth. The texture should resemble smooth pudding after being blended on high. Put everything in a big basin and stir it up. Sift the cocoa powder, baking soda, almond flour, and coconut flour into a large mixing basin. Combine the ingredients well. Combine the avocado and almond milk and stir to combine. In a separate bowl, whisk together the flour and salt, then add it to the avocado combination and fold until everything is incorporated. Don't beat the mixture to death. Blend in the blueberries and chocolate chips. Spoon the mixture equally into the 9 prepared muffin cups. Put in the oven and cook for approximately 18 minutes. Do not eat the muffins too warm.

Nutrition Calories: 130 Kcal, Proteins: 10.4g, Fat: 5g, Carbohydrates: 11g

2.7 Tropical Smoothie Bowl
Preparation time: 15 Minutes **Cooking time:** 0 Minutes **Serving:** 2 Persons

Ingredients

- 1 cup orange juice
- 1 cup pineapple (frozen)
- 1 cup mango (frozen)
- 1/2 banana
- 1 spoonful of chia

- 1/8 teaspoon turmeric

Toppings:

- Kiwis (sliced)
- Coconut flakes
- Almonds (chopped)
- Strawberries (sliced)

Instructions. Place everything into a blender and mix until smooth. Put them in a blender and whirl them around until they form a smooth cream. If the mixture is excessively thick, a few drops of oranges at a time can do the trick. Split the smoothie in half and serve it in separate bowls. Blend the ingredients together and serve in individual bowls. Serve.

Nutrition Calories: 230 Kcal, Proteins: 11.4g, Fat: 5g, Carbohydrates: 35g

2.8 Smoked Salmon in Scrambled Eggs

Preparation time: 10 Minutes **Cooking time:** 0 Minutes **Serving:** 1 Person

Ingredients

- 4 eggs
- 4 slices of smoked salmon (chopped)
- 3 stems of fresh chives (finely chopped)
- Pinch of sea salt
- 2 tablespoons coconut milk
- Pinch of black pepper (freshly ground)
- Cooking fat

Instructions. Coconut milk, chives, and eggs should all be combined in a large bowl. Blend them with a whisk. Put salt and pepper on it. Beat the eggs in enough grease in a pan over medium heat. The eggs should be poured into the pan. Scramble the eggs by stirring them. Scramble the eggs and add the fish. Add additional 2 minutes to the cooking time. Serve.

Nutrition Calories: 205 Kcal, Proteins: 18.4g, Fat: 0.5g, Carbohydrates: 2.3g

2.9 Spinach and Potatoes with Smoked Salmon

Preparation time: 10 Minutes **Cooking time:** 0 Minutes **Serving:** 1 Person

Ingredients

- 2 russet potatoes (peeled and diced)
- 4 eggs
- 1/2 onion (sliced)
- 2 cups baby spinach (fresh)
- 8 ounces smoked salmon (sliced)

- 1/2 cup mushrooms (sliced)
- 2 tablespoons olive oil
- 1 garlic clove (minced)
- 2 tablespoons ghee
- 1/2 teaspoon garlic powder
- 1/2 teaspoon onion powder
- 1/4 teaspoon paprika
- Black pepper
- Sea salt

Instructions Turn the oven temperature up to 425 degrees F. To prepare a baking dish, line it with parchment paper. Arrange the potatoes on the prepared baking sheet. Sprinkle paprika, olive oil, onion powder, and garlic powder over the potatoes. Put pepper on it. Russet potatoes need thirty minutes in the oven. At the halfway point, give the potatoes a flip. Put some water in a saucepan and set it over high heat. Let the water boil. Prepare a pot of boiling water for the eggs. Remove the heat source. Leave the eggs in the heated water for Seven minutes.

Remove the eggs from the cooker. The eggs should be rinsed under running water. Prepare the eggs by removing the shells. Place the ghee in a pot and melt it over medium heat. In a skillet, heat the oil and sauté the garlic and onion for a few seconds. Place the mushrooms inside. Put salt and pepper on it. Add another 5 minutes to the cooking time. Prepare the spinach and add it. Let them cook for 2 minutes or till they are crumpled. Cut the brown potatoes into quarters and serve them evenly. Pile smoked salmon on top of the eggs and spinach combination.

Nutrition Calories: 205 Kcal, Proteins: 6g, Fat: 2.1g, Carbohydrates: 2.3g

2.10 Eggs in a Mushroom and Bacon
Preparation time: 10 Minutes **Cooking time:** 0 Minutes **Serving:** 4 Persons

Ingredients

- 4 Portobello mushroom caps
- 4 pasture-raised eggs (large)
- 2 strips thick-cut and pasture-raised bacon (cooked and chopped)
- 1 cup arugula
- 1 medium tomato (chopped)
- Pepper
- Salt

Instructions. Set the oven temperature to 350 degrees F. So, have a baking sheet ready. Put parchment paper in it. Use a spoon to remove the heads from the mushrooms. Throw the gills away. Place the mushroom caps in a single layer on the prepared baking sheet. Put some arugula and diced tomatoes in each mushroom cap and serve. Put an egg over mushroom stems very carefully. Put the mushrooms in the center of the oven and bake for 20 minutes.

Put some bacon, salt, and pepper, on top of each mushroom. Serve.

Nutrition Calories: 124 Kcal, Proteins: 8g, Fat: 8.4g, Carbohydrates: 4.3g

2.11 Bacon Avocado Burger

Preparation time: 10 Minutes **Cooking time:** 0 Minutes **Serving:** 1 Person

Ingredients

- 1 ripe avocado
- 2 bacon rashers
- 1 red onion (sliced)
- 1 lettuce leaf
- 1 egg
- Sea salt
- 1 tomato (sliced)
- Sesame seeds (for garnishing)
- 1 tablespoon Paleo mayonnaise

Instructions. Carefully place the bacon in the pan. To preheat the stove, set the temperature to medium. Brown the bacon. Whenever the bacon rashers flare, flip them with a fork. Keep frying until they reach the desired crispiness. Don't eat any more of that deliciously crispy bacon right now. Break the egg into the same pan you used to cook the bacon. Make a fried egg in bacon grease. It is ideal for the egg white to be firm but the yolk to be soft. Put the finished egg to one side. You should halve the avocado lengthwise. Dig that hole out! Remove the meat by spooning it out of the skin. Spread the mayonnaise into the empty space left by the avocado. Spread the avocado on a plate, and then layer on the bacon, egg, tomato, and onion. Sprinkle some salt over it. Complete the layer by slicing the remaining avocado in half and spreading it on top. Sprinkle some sesame seeds on top. Serve.

Nutrition Calories: 440 Kcal, Proteins: 37g, Fat: 49g, Carbohydrates: 51g

2.12 Spinach Fry Up & Tomato Mushroom

Preparation time: 10 Minutes **Cooking time:** 5 Minutes **Serving:** 2 Persons

Ingredients

- 3 large handfuls of English spinach leaves (torn)
- 6 button mushrooms (sliced)
- A handful of cherry tomatoes (sliced in halves)
- 1 garlic clove (finely diced)
- Drizzle of lemon juice
- 1/2 red onion (sliced)
- 2 tablespoons olive oil

- 1/2 teaspoon lemon zest (grated)
- 1 teaspoon ghee
- 1/2 teaspoon sea salt
- Pinch of black pepper (ground)
- Pinch of nutmeg

Instructions. Put the olive oil and ghee in a pan and heat them over medium heat. The mushrooms and onions should be cooked in a sautéing pan until tender. Tomatoes, lemon, and garlic rind should be combined and stirred together. Add some salt, pepper, and nutmeg for flavor. Add additional 2 minutes to the cooking time. Make the minced tomato sauce by mashing tomatoes with a spatula. Add the spinach leaves and mix. Wilt them in the cooking process. Put some lime juice on it. Serve.

Nutrition Calories: 61.5 Kcal, Proteins: 3.3g, Fat: 2.5g, Carbohydrates: 6.6g

2.13 Papaya smoothie
Ingredients
- 1 papaya
- 1 carrot
- ½ mango
- ½ banana
- One-inch piece of ginger
- 1 tablespoon pumpkin seeds
- 1 heaping tablespoon of yogurt
- ½ teaspoon of turmeric
- ¾ cup orange juice
- Ice

Instructions. Put all the ingredients in a blender or a shaker except the ice. Beat until you have a creamy mixture. Serve with ice cubes or crushed ice.

2.14 Aricot Lassi
Ingredients
- 1 cup Greek yogurt
- 2 cups water (remove if you like it more solid)
- 1 + 1/2 ripe banana
- 5 pitted apricots
- 1/2 tsp Vanilla Flavored Oatmeal Powder
- 1/2 tsp cardamom powder
- 2 tsp honey
- 2 tsp grated fresh ginger
- 1/2 lemon (in juice)
- 1 pinch salt

Instructions. Put all the ingredients in the blender glass. Beat until creamy.

2.15 Stuffed pineapple

Ingredients

- 1 frozen banana
- ¼ cup non-dairy milk
- ½ small avocado
- 2 handfuls of baby spinach
- ½ pineapple (to use as a container)
- ¾ cup fresh pineapple chunks
- 1 teaspoon flax seeds
- For decoration
- Pumpkin and sunflower seeds
- Raspberries

Instructions. Cut the pineapple in two and carefully hollow out the inside. Reserve the shell, as it will be the bowl for this dish. Put the peeled frozen banana, milk, diced avocado, washed bones, pineapple chunks (leave some for garnish), and flaxseeds into a blender or mixer and blend on high speed. Pour the mixture into the pineapple skin when you get a creamy texture. Decorate with raspberries, small pieces of pineapple, coconut slices, and pumpkin seeds.

2.16 Turmeric herbal tea

Ingredients

- 1 cup of boiling water
- ½ tablespoon of turmeric powder
- 1 tablespoon of fresh ginger, thinly sliced
- 1 handful of cilantro, chopped
- 2 lemons squeezed
- 1 clove of garlic, peeled and crushed
- 1 tablespoon of olive oil
- 5 peppercorns, whole
- 1 orange (or 1½ tablespoons of honey)

Instructions. Boil the water on the stove, then add all the ingredients and leave to macerate for 10 minutes. Strain in a colander and finally enjoy!

2.17 Herbal tea with milk, whiskey, honey, cinnamon, and turmeric

Ingredients

- 1 cup of fresh milk (or pasteurized milk)
- 1 tablespoon of honey
- 1/2 glass of whiskey, depending on tolerance!
- 1/4 teaspoon cinnamon (optional)
- 1/4 teaspoon of turmeric

Instructions. Heat the milk, honey, whiskey, and other ingredients over medium heat until they foam. Finally, pour it into a cup and enjoy!

2.18 Turmeric Crackers

Ingredients

- 300 g of type 1 or 2 flour
- 70 ml of extra virgin olive oil
- 50 ml of water
- 50 ml of wine or white or red
- 2 teaspoons of turmeric
- 2 pinches of salt
- 1 pinch of paprika
- 1 pinch of pepper
- a handful of sesame seeds
- 1 teaspoon full of mixed herbs

Instructions. In a bowl, pour the sifted flour, water, oil, and wine, mix all the ingredients, and add the turmeric, sesame, salt, spicy paprika, pepper, and aromatic herbs. Knead well until the dough is homogeneous and smooth, cover the dough, and let it rest for 15-20 minutes. Preheat the oven to 180 degrees, roll out the dough until you get a rectangular layer, and cut to the size you prefer. Bake for 20 minutes, and finally, enjoy!

2.19 Cauliflower in cream cheese

Prep Time: 15 minutes **Cook Time:** 10 minutes **Total Time:** 25 minutes

Servings: 5

Ingredients

- 1 cauliflower
- 250 ml of milk
- 100 gr of grated Parmesan cheese
- 2 tablespoons of corn
- 1 yolk
- Enough of nutmeg
- Enough of salt

Instructions. First, wash the cauliflower, put it in a pot with plenty of salted water, turn on the fire and let it boil. Now butter a dripping pan, drain the cauliflower, and spread it inside, letting it rest to cool for a few minutes. Now pour the milk into a small pan, boil it, season with nutmeg and salt, then mix everything properly. Separately, melt the cornstarch in cold water, then add it to the milk and when it is about to boil, turn off the stove. Continue to mix so that the ingredients bind, then add the egg, and once you have a smooth cream, add the Parmesan and salt. Once this is done, once the consistency of the cream cheese is satisfactory, pour it over your cauliflowers. Finally, cook it in a preheated oven for 10 minutes at a temperature of 220 ° C; at the end, bring it to the table.

2.20 Barley Water

Working time: 1 hour 20 minutes **Completed in:** 2 hrs 20 mins **Calories:** 57

Servings: 4

Ingredients

- Barley 60 grams

- Water 1½ liters / 1500g
- Cinammon 2 pinch / 2 g
- Salt 1 pinch / 1 g
- Honey 1 teaspoon / 8g
- lemon (organic) 2 tablespoons / 10g

Instructions. Boil the barley in 1 liter of water and simmer for 1 hour. Add other ingredients, such as cinnamon, salt, and honey, and cook for another 5 minutes. Strain the barley water through a sieve, collecting the barley water and allowing it to cool. After cooling, add lemon juice-done. This healing drink from England tastes good and can also replace a meal during a diet, give athletes strength, protect against colds, or -similar to oatmeal- calm the stomach or intestines.

2.21 Bread with avocado and egg
Preparation: 25 mins **Calories:** 325 kcal **Servings:** 4
Ingredients
- 200g _ kale
- salt
- 30g _ stoned green olives
- 1 clove of garlic
- 2 spring onions
- 1 tbsp lemon juice
- 1 tbsp olive oil
- 40ml _ vegetable broth
- Pepper
- 20g _ pine nuts (1 tbsp)
- 1 avocado
- 4 discs
- whole grain bread
- 2 tbsp white wine vinegar
- 4 eggs
- 2 tbsp red cress
- 1 tbsp chive rolls
- 3g _ chia seeds (1 tsp)

Instructions. Clean, wash and coarsely chop the kale. Blanch in boiling salted water for about 5 minutes. Then remove, rinse in cold water, drain and chop very finely. Meanwhile, chop the olives very finely; Clean, wash, and finely chop the garlic and spring onions, mix with the kale, and toss with the lemon juice, oil, and broth. Season with salt and pepper. Roast the pine nuts without fat and let them cool down. Halve the avocado, remove the stone, remove the flesh from the skin and cut it into wedges. Toast the bread slices in a toaster. Bring water to a boil with salt and vinegar. Crack the eggs, one at a time, into a soup ladle and gently slide them into the broth. Let it simmer for about 4-5 minutes over medium heat. Top the bread slices with avocado wedges, add 1 egg, and the kale-olive paste to each. Sprinkle with pine nuts, cress, chives, and chia seeds.

2.22 Turmeric water

Working time: 5 mins **Completed in:** 15 minutes **Calories:** 18 **Servings:** 4

Ingredients

- Water 1 liter / 1000g
- Turmeric 1 teaspoon / 1g
- Pepper 1 pinch / 1 g
- Ginger 1 piece / 5g
- Orange 1 piece / 150g

Instructions. Put water in a saucepan and heat. Peel a piece of ginger (about 3-4cm) and chop finely. Stir the ginger pieces, turmeric, and pepper into the water and bring to a boil. Lower the heat and simmer for about 10 minutes. Squeeze orange. When the turmeric water has cooled, stir in the fresh orange juice. The turmeric water can also be enjoyed as a healthy lemonade with ice cubes.

2.23 Swedish milk potato vegetable soup

Working time: 15 minutes. **Completed in:** 35 mins **Calories:** 436 **Servings:** 2

Ingredients

- Potatoes 400 grams
- cucumber/s 1 piece / 550g
- radish 15 pieces / 175 g
- dill (fresh) something / 10 g
- parsley (fresh) something / 10 g
- Swedish milk 500 milliliters
- chia oil 2 tablespoons / 16g
- water 300 milliliters
- Salt
- Black pepper

Instructions. For the cold Swedish milk soup, peel the potatoes, wash them, and cut them into small cubes. Bring lightly salted water to a boil in a saucepan and cook the potato pieces for 20 minutes. Drain and let cool. In the meantime, wash the radishes and cucumbers thoroughly and dice finely. Wash, dry, and finely chop the dill and parsley. Mix Swedish milk with chia oil, cold water, and lightly salt and pepper. Stir in the radishes, cucumber, parsley, dill, and the cooled potato pieces, and refrigerate until ready to serve. The healthy probiotic meal with Swedish milk is ready.

2.24 Almond porridge with blueberries

Preparation: 15 minutes **Calories:** 442 kcal **Servings:** 4

Ingredients

- 800ml _ almond drink (almond milk)
- 200g _ tender oatmeal
- 4 tsp maple syrup
- 120g _ blueberries
- 50g _ unpeeled almonds (4 tbsp)
- 20g _ amaranth pops (4 tsp)
- 60g _ almond butter (4 tbsp)

Instructions. Heat the almond drink in a saucepan. Stir in the oatmeal and maple syrup and simmer over medium heat for 2-3 minutes. Then let it simmer for about 5 minutes over low heat. Meanwhile, wash the blueberries and pat dry. Roughly chop the almonds. Pour the porridge into glasses or bowls and serve with blueberries, almonds, puffed amaranth and almond butter.

2.25 Chocolate Milkshake

Preparation time: 12 Minutes **Cooking time:** 5 Minutes **Serving:** 2 Persons

Ingredients

- 4 ice cubes
- 2 large organic bananas (frozen)
- 1/2 teaspoon vanilla extract
- 1 cup coconut milk
- 2 tablespoons cashew butter
- 1 tablespoon cacao powder (raw)

Instructions. Put the coconut cream and bananas in a blender or food processor and blend until smooth. Double or triple pulse. Stir in the cocoa powder, nut butter, and flavoring. Repeat the process two or three times. Fill it up with ice. Put everything in a blender and whir it up until it's completely combined. The consistency of the milkshake may be adjusted to taste by adding additional ice cubes or coconut milk. Fill a glass with it. Serve.

Nutrition Calories: 371 Kcal, Proteins: 8.2g, Fat: 17g, Carbohydrates: 51g

2.26 Almond Sweet Cherry Chia Pudding

Preparation time: 15 Minutes **Cooking time:** Minutes **Serving:** 2 Persons

Ingredients

- 2 cups whole sweet cherries (pitted)
- 3/4 cup chia seeds
- 1/2 cup hemp seeds
- 1/4 cup maple syrup
- 13.5 ounces can coconut milk
- 1 teaspoon vanilla extract
- 1 teaspoon almond extract
- 1/8 teaspoon sea salt

Topping:

- four servings of cherry

Instructions. The cherries, vanilla extract, coconut milk, almond extract, salt, and maple syrup should be blended together. They should be blended until they are completely smooth. Add the chia seeds and hemp seeds. Put everything in the blender and mix on a low speed to combine.

Divide it across 4 glasses. Allow the pudding to chill in the refrigerator for a minimum of an hour. Cherry, each pudding to finish it off. Serve.

Nutrition Calories: 242 Kcal, Proteins: 7g, Fat: 11g, Carbohydrates: 33g

2.27 Shakshuka

Preparation time: 10 Minutes **Serving:** 6 Persons

Ingredients

- 6 eggs (large)
- 4 cups tomatoes (diced)
- 1/2 onion (chopped)
- Sea salt
- 1 clove of garlic (minced)
- 1 red bell pepper (chopped and seeded)
- 2 tablespoons tomato paste
- 1/2 tablespoon fresh parsley (finely chopped)
- 1 tablespoon cooking fat
- 1 teaspoon paprika
- Pinch of cayenne pepper
- 1 teaspoon chili powder
- Black pepper

Instructions. Place the lard for frying in a pan and heat it over medium heat. For two minutes, sauté the onions. The garlic should be added now. The onions should be sautéed until they are soft. Add the bell pepper and mix well. Wait until the chills are tender before serving. Tomatoes, chili powder, paprika, cayenne pepper, and tomato paste should be stirred in. Add salt and pepper to taste. Temper the heat a little. The ingredients should be heated for several minutes at a low simmer. The eggs should be broken over the mixture while it is still boiling. Spread the eggs out equally. Keep the skillet covered. Keep it at a heat till the eggs are done. Top with chopped parsley. Serve.

Nutrition Calories: 298 Kcal, Proteins: 17g, Fat: 19g, Carbohydrates: 16g

2.28 Anti-Inflammatory Salad

Preparation time: 12 Minutes **Serving:** 4 Persons

Ingredients

Dressing:

- 1 clove of garlic (grated)
- 1/3 cup extra virgin olive oil
- 2 tablespoons apple cider vinegar

- 1 tablespoon lemon juice
- 1 teaspoon turmeric
- 1 teaspoon fresh ginger (grated)
- 1/2 teaspoon sea salt
- 1/4 teaspoon black pepper (freshly ground)

Salad:

- 16 ounces beets (cooked, peeled, and chopped)
- 2 12-ounce bags of Trader Joe's Sweet Kale Salad Mix
- 1 1/2 cup blueberries (fresh)

Instructions. Put the dressing components in a blender and mix until smooth. The salad components should be split between six bowls. Dress with a drizzle. Serve.

Nutrition Calories: 20 Kcal, Proteins: 17g, Fat: 19g, Carbohydrates: 16g

2.29 Amaranth Porridge with Pears

Preparation time: 12 Minutes **Cooking time:** 5 Minutes **Serving:** 4 Persons

Ingredients

Pears:

- 1 teaspoon maple syrup
- 1 pear (large and diced)
- 1/2 teaspoon cinnamon (ground)
- 1/4 teaspoon ginger (ground)
- 1/8 teaspoon nutmeg (ground)
- 1/8 teaspoon clove (ground)

Porridge:

- 1/2 cup amaranth (uncooked, drained, and rinsed)
- 1/2 cup water
- 1 cup 2% milk
- 1/4 teaspoon salt

Topping:

- 1 cup 0% Greek yogurt (plain)
- 2 tablespoons pecan pieces
- 1 teaspoon maple syrup (pure)

Instructions. Turn the oven temperature up to 400 degrees F. Prepare parchment paper on a baking pan. Put all of the porridge components into a saucepan and cook them over medium. Get the water boiling? Turn down the stove. Allow the porridge to cook for a quarter of an hour.

Putting aside. The pecan bits should be spread out on the prepared baking sheet. Spread maple syrup all over them. On the same baking sheet coated with pecan bits, place the diced pears. Pour some maple syrup over the pears. Bake them in the microwave for fifteen minutes. Stir the fruits into the cereal. Keep some pears for sprinkling. Two cups of porridge, please. Put some yogurt in each of the dishes. Porridge should be served in bowls. Add the remaining pears and pecans to the top of each serving of porridge. Serve.

Nutrition Calories: 500 Kcal, Proteins: 78g, Fat: 1.5g, Carbohydrates: 8g

2.30 Sweet Potato Breakfast Bowl

Preparation time: 15 Minutes **Cooking time:** 5 Minutes **Serving:** 3 Persons

Ingredients

- 1 small banana (sliced)
- 1 small sweet potato (pre-baked)
- 1/4 cup raspberries
- 1 serving protein powder
- 1/4 cup blueberries

Toppings:

- Favorite nuts
- Chia seeds
- Cacao nibs
- Hemp hearts

Instructions. Purée the sweet potato in a bowl. Add the protein powder and mix well. Mix. Arrange the bananas, raspberries, and blueberries on top. Sprinkle on the condiments after. Serve.

Nutrition Calories: 210 Kcal, Proteins: 3.8g, Fat: 1.3g, Carbohydrates: 48g

2.31 Apple Turkey Hash

Preparation time: 20 Minutes **Cooking time:** 0 Minutes **Serving:** 4 Persons

Ingredients

Hash:

- 2 cups spinach
- 2 cups frozen butternut squash (cubed)
- 1/2 cup carrots (shredded)
- 1 large apple (peeled, cored, and chopped)
- 1 onion
- 1 large zucchini
- 1 teaspoon cinnamon

- 1 tablespoon coconut oil

- 1/2 teaspoon thyme (dried)

- 1/2 teaspoon garlic powder

- 1/2 teaspoon turmeric

- 3/4 teaspoon powdered ginger

- Sea salt

Meat:

- 1/2 teaspoon thyme (dried)

- 1 pound ground turkey

- 1 tablespoon coconut oil

- 1/2 teaspoon cinnamon

- Sea salt

Instructions. Put the coconut oil in a pan and heat it over medium heat. When the turkey is done, add it to the pan and stir it in. Add some salt, pepper, cinnamon, and thyme to taste. Putting aside. Toss the coconut oil into the same pan and heat it over moderate heat. Lighten the onions by sautéing them. Mix in the apples, butternut squash, carrots, and zucchini. Make sure they're cooked all the way through so they're nice and tender. Blend in the spinach. If you want it wilted, cook it longer. Add the minced turkey and mix it with the other ingredients. Serve.

Nutrition Calories: 325 Kcal, Proteins: 28g, Fat: 19g, Carbohydrates: 20g

2.32 Oats with Almonds and Blueberries

Preparation time: 15 Minutes **Cooking time:** 0 Minutes **Serving:** 4 Persons

Ingredients

Oats:

- 3/4 cup old-fashioned oats

- 3/4 cup almond milk

- 1 tablespoon maple syrup

Toppings:

- 1/4 cup blueberries

- 1/3 cup yogurt

- 3 tablespoons almonds (sliced)

Instructions. Scoop the oats into a canning jar (1-pint). Combine the almond milk and maple syrup well in a bowl. Mix the milk and honey into the oats. Lock the lid on the jar. Reserve in the refrigerator for at least eight hours, preferably overnight. Fill it with condiments. Serve.

Nutrition Calories: 230 Kcal, Proteins: 8g, Fat: 5g, Carbohydrates: 40g

2.33 Chia Energy Bars with Chocolate

Preparation time: 12 Minutes **Cooking time:** 0 Minutes **Serving:** 4 Persons

Ingredients

- 1 cup walnut pieces (raw)
- 1 1/2 cups pitted dates (packed)
- 1/3 cup cacao powder (raw)
- 1/2 cup whole chia seeds
- 1/2 cup coconut shavings
- 1 teaspoon pure vanilla extract
- 1/2 cup dark chocolate (chopped)
- 1/4 teaspoon sea salt (unrefined)
- 1/2 cup oats

Instructions. Place the dates into the food processor. Prepare a thick paste by processing. Place it in a basin for mixing. Drop the walnuts in there. Ensure an in-depth blending. Add the last of the ingredients. Knead it until it creates a ball of dough. Obtain a square dish for baking. Prepare the dish by lining it with baking parchment. Place the mixture on the prepared baking sheet. Evenly disperse the dough, and then push it down firmly into the dish. Freeze for at least a few hours and up to a full day. Cube into 14 pieces. Serve.

Nutrition Calories: 234 Kcal, Proteins: 4.5g, Fat: 12g, Carbohydrates: 28g

---

2.34 Baked Rice Porridge with Maple and Fruit

Preparation time: 15 Minutes **Cooking time:** 0 Minutes **Serving:** 5 Persons

Ingredients

- 2 tablespoons pure maple syrup
- 1/2 cup brown rice
- 1/2 teaspoon pure vanilla extract
- Pinch of cinnamon
- Sliced fruits (berries, plums, pears, or cherries)
- Pinch of salt

Instructions. Turn the oven temperature up to 400 degrees F. Brown rice and a glass of water should be cooked together in a saucepan over moderate heat. Get the water boiling. Blend with some vanilla bean paste and cinnamon. Cover. Turn down the stove. Allow the rice to boil until it is done. Toss the rice every once in a while. Have two bowls that can go from fridge to oven ready. Assign each bowl the same amount of rice. Sprinkle some maple syrup and sliced fruits over the rice. Put some salt on it. Put in the oven and set the timer for 15 minutes. Serve.

Nutrition Calories: 228 Kcal, Proteins: 3.5g, Fat: 1.5g, Carbohydrates: 50g

2.35 Banana Chia Pudding

Preparation time: 20 Minutes **Cooking time:** 0 Minutes **Serving:** 5 Persons

Ingredients

- 1/2 cup chia seeds
- 2 cups almond milk (unsweetened)
- 1 large banana (very ripe)
- 1/2 teaspoon pure vanilla extract
- 2 tablespoon maple syrup
- 1 tablespoon cacao powder

Mix-ins:

- 2 tablespoons chocolate chips
- 2 tablespoons cacao nibs
- 1 large banana (sliced)

Instructions. Put the banana and chia seeds in a large bowl and stir them together. Combine the ingredients by mashing them well. Combine the milk and vanilla essence and add to the pan. Mix well to eliminate any lumps. Get two sealed containers ready. To divide the chia seeds in half, divide the mixture between two containers. Cover. The remaining portion of the hemp seeds combination should be combined with maple syrup and cacao powder. Make sure everything is well combined. Transfer the compound to the secondary container. Cover. These containers should be refrigerated for at least a few hours, preferably overnight. Divide the chia pudding and the toppings into 3 glasses and layer. Serve.

Nutrition Calories: 260 Kcal, Proteins: 6g, Fat: 5g, Carbohydrates: 60g

2.36 Baked Eggs with Herbs

Preparation time: 15 Minutes **Cooking time:** 10 Minutes **Serving:** 5 Persons

Ingredients

- A tablespoon of milk
- A sprinkling of dried herbs like thyme, oregano, parsley, garlic powder, and dill
- A teaspoon of melted butter,
- Two eggs

Instructions. Turn the oven's broiler on to a low level and preheat it. Put the butter and milk in a medium baking dish. Combo together successfully. Spread the butter-milk combo all over the baking dish. Separate the eggs and place them in the dish. Top with a sprinkling of herbs and garlic. Put it in the oven for a couple of minutes so the eggs can bake.

Nutrition Calories: 341 Kcal, Proteins: 20g, Fat: 27g, Carbohydrates: 3g

2.37 Smoothie Bowl with Raspberries

Servings: 2 **Preparation time**: 5 minutes

Ingredients

- 150 g of raspberries + 3-4 for decoration
- 200 g of Greek yogurt
- 1 banana
- 2 tablespoons of honey
- 2 tablespoons of oat flakes or granola without sugar
- 1 tablespoon of chia seeds
- 1 tablespoon of dried blueberries
- 2 spoons of toasted sliced almonds

Instructions. In a bowl, blend the raspberries, banana, yogurt, honey, and dried blueberries. Pour the mixture into bowls and decorate with raspberries, chia seeds, toasted almonds, oat flakes, or granola.

2.38 Tigernut Waffles

Working time: 25 mins **Completed in**: 25 mins **Calories:** 554 **Servings:** 2

Ingredients

- Tigernut Flour 75 grams
- Oatmeal (gluten free) 125 grams
- Natural oat milk 150 milliliters
- Cinammon 1 pinch / 1 g
- Water 70 grams
- Coconut oil 3 tablespoons / 25g

Instructions. Finely grind the oat flakes with a smoothie maker or in a grain mill. Add the tiger nut flour, oat milk, 2 tbsp coconut oil, water, and cinnamon, and mix well. Let the dough swell for 10 minutes, and then add a little water if necessary. The batter should be quite runny so that the waffle batter spreads well and the waffles stay light and fluffy. Preheat the waffle iron and brush both sides thinly with coconut oil using a brush. Place the oatmeal and tigernut waffle batter in the center of the waffle iron and spread evenly. Close the waffle iron and bake each waffle for about 3 minutes until golden. Homemade apple sauce or berry sauce goes well with this. The waffle batter is enough for about 4 waffles, i.e., 2 healthy waffles per person.

2.39 Barley Grass Strawberry Smoothie

Working time: 15 minutes. **Completed in:** 15 minutes. **Calories:** 148 **Servings:** 2

Ingredients

- Strawberries (frozen) 50 grams
- Kale (frozen) 50 grams
- cucumber/s ½ piece / 250 g
- banana 1 piece / 155g
- Barley Grass Juice Powder 2 teaspoons / 8g
- hemp seeds (shelled) 1 tablespoon / 12g
- Water 100 milliliters

Instructions

Put the strawberries and kale (frozen) in the blender or wash and drain fresh ones beforehand. Wash the cucumber and cut it into pieces and add. Add hemp seeds, barley grass powder, and water and mix thoroughly in a blender on high to form a smoothie. Without frozen food, you can also use a hand blender. Pour into two tall glasses and serve. Other berries (e.g., raspberries, currants) also work, and instead of kale, lettuce also tastes good. You can increase the amount of barley grass powder as you wish. Strong immune system: This smoothie has (especially due to the barley grass powder) a lot of calcium, iron, vitamin B1, vitamin C, and zinc, and due to the hemp seeds, many healthy fatty acids.

2.40 Chia pudding with linseed oil

Preparation: 20 min **Ready in:** 12 hours 40 minutes **Calories:** 200 kcal **Servings:** 4

Ingredients

- 350ml _ unsweetened almond drink (almond milk)
- 1 pinch vanilla powder
- 60g _ chia seeds
- 300g _ small papaya (1 small papaya)
- 40g _ dried soft apricot
- 1 tbsp lemon juice
- 1 tbsp linseed oil
- 20g _ walnut kernels (1 heaped tbsp)

Instructions. Mix the almond drink, vanilla, and chia seeds, leave to swell for about 20 minutes, and stir again. Divide the chia pudding into 4 glasses and cover, and place in the fridge for 12 hours, preferably overnight. The next day, deseed the papaya and cut the flesh into bite-sized pieces. Cut the apricots into small cubes. Mix the fruit with the lemon juice and linseed oil and leave to stand for about 10 minutes. Meanwhile, roughly chop the walnuts. Put the papaya and apricot mixture in the glasses on top of the chia pudding and sprinkle with the nuts.

2.41 Fruit salad with nuts

Working time: 2 min **Completed in:** 4 min **Calories:** 327 **Servings:** 2

Ingredients

- organic apple 1 piece / 150g
- strawberries 100 gram
- orange 150 grams

- hazelnuts 10pcs /20g
- Flaxseed (crushed) 1 tablespoon / 15g
- Walnuts 4 pieces / 25g
- linseed oil (native) 1 teaspoon / 5g
- Omega 3 algae oil 1 teaspoon / 5g

Instructions. Wash the fruit, remove the core or peel and cut it into bite-sized pieces. Chop the nuts. Stir linseed, algae oil, linseed, and chopped nuts into the fruit salad. Finished! You can vary the types of fruit as you wish.

2.42 Avocado Grapefruit Salad with Quinoa

Preparation: 35 mins **Calories:** 336 kcal **Servings:** 4

Ingredients

- 150g _ quinoa
- salt
- 2 grapefruits
- 7g _ dijon mustard (1 tsp)
- 2 tsp honey
- 2 tbsp olive oil
- pepper
- 2 boxes cress
- 1 avocado
- 1 bunch spring onions

Instructions. Cook the quinoa twice the amount of boiling salted water for about 20 minutes, drain, and leave to cool for 10 minutes. Meanwhile, peel the grapefruits with a knife thick enough to remove the white inner skin. Cut out the grapefruit fillets between the membranes, catching the dripping juice. Mix the juice with mustard, honey, and oil, and season with salt and pepper. Cut the cress from the bed. Clean and wash the spring onions and cut them diagonally into rings. Halve and seed the avocado, lift the flesh out of the bowl and cut into slices. Mix all the prepared salad ingredients with the dressing and arrange on plates.

2.43 Smoothie bowl

Working time: 10 mins **Completed in:** 10 mins **Calories:** 228 **Servings:** 2

Ingredients

- Banana 1 piece / 115g
- blueberries (frozen) 200 grams
- coconut yogurt 3 tablespoons / 45g
- almond milk (no additives) 100 milliliters
- oatmeal 2 tablespoons / 12g
- Goji berries 2 teaspoons / 10g
- Chia seeds 2 teaspoons / 6g
- pumpkin seeds 2 teaspoons / 10g
- sunflower seeds 2 teaspoons / 10g
- soft fruit 2 tablespoons / 20g

Instructions. Peel and coarsely chop the banana. Pour into an oblong container (about a measuring cup). Also, add the frozen blueberries, coconut yogurt, oat flakes, almond milk, and puree everything with a hand blender to a creamy mass. Add more liquid if necessary. Divide between 2 bowls and place 1 teaspoon of chia seeds, sunflower seeds, pumpkin seeds, goji berries, and other berries in the smoothie bowl. Your vitamin breakfast is ready!

2.44 Chia pudding with raspberries and coconut flakes

Working time: 15 minutes. **Completed in:** 1 hour 15 minutes **Calories:** 216 **Servings**: 2
Ingredients

- almond milk (no additives) 300 milliliters
- Chia seeds 3 tablespoons / 30g
- Raspberries 125 grams
- coconut flakes 20 g
- honey 1 tablespoon / 20g

Instructions. Divide the chia seeds, almond milk, and honey evenly between two glasses or dessert bowls and stir. Chill (refrigerator) for about 1 hour. Stir from time to time so that the chia seeds are evenly distributed and do not stick too much together. Spread the fresh raspberries on the finished chia pudding and top with coconut flakes. Tastes delicious as a light dessert. Very healthy!

2.45 Iced Matcha Tea

Ingredients

- 1 or 2 tbsp matcha tea
- 1 cup macadamia nut milk
- 1 cup of ice
- 1 cda honey
- 1 cda superfoods recovery
- For the homemade macadamia nut milk
- 1 cup macadamia nuts
- 1 + 1/2 cup of water

Instructions. For the homemade macadamia nut milk Put the nuts and water in the blender. We beat at high speed. Strain through a strainer or mesh so there are no lumps or different textures. For the iced tea add the milk that we just made along with the other ingredients. We beat at high speed. We serve and voila!

2.46 Lentil and Barley Salad

Preparation: 45 mins **Calories:** 619 kcal **Servings:** 4
Ingredients

- 300g _ beetroot (2)
- 6 tbsp olive oil
- salt
- pepper
- 240g _ beluga lentils

- 75g _ pearl barley
- 1 clove of garlic
- 15g _ hazelnut kernels (1 tbsp)
- 1 bunch radish
- 80g _ rocket (1 bunch)
- 4 stems mint
- 70g _ celery (1 stalk)
- 200g _ feta (45% fat in dry matter)
- 1 tbsp walnut oil
- 1 pinch ground allspice
- 1 pinch cayenne pepper
- 2 tbsp lemon juice

Instructions. Clean the beetroot, peel, cut into slices and place on a baking tray lined with baking paper. Drizzle with 2 tbsp olive oil, salt and pepper. Cook in a preheated oven at 180 °C (convection oven 160 °C; gas: level 2-3) for 35 minutes until soft. Then take it out. Meanwhile, rinse the lentils and pearl barley in a colander. Cook in a saucepan of boiling salted water for 30 minutes until al dente. Pour into a colander, drain and leave to cool. Meanwhile, peel and halve the garlic. Roughly chop the hazelnuts. Clean, wash and slice the radishes. Wash the arugula and mint and shake dry. Clean, wash and thinly slice the celery. Crumble feta.

Halve the beetroot slices and finely puree with a hand blender with 2 tablespoons of olive oil, walnut oil, garlic, hazelnuts, salt, allspice and cayenne pepper. Season the beetroot puree with salt and pepper. Mix the lemon juice with the remaining oil, salt and pepper. Arrange the lentils and pearl barley with the beetroot puree, rocket, mint, celery, radishes and feta and drizzle with the dressing.

2.47 Flea seed yogurt with berries

Working time: 10 mins **Completed in:** 10 mins **Calories:** 221 **Servings:** 2

Ingredients

- Coconut yogurt 300 grams
- Flea seed shells, ground 1 tablespoon / 3g
- Chia seeds 1 teaspoon / 3g
- Hemp seeds (shelled) 1 teaspoon / 5g
- Strawberries 100 gram
- Blueberries 100 gram
- Coconut flakes 1 tablespoon / 5g

Instructions. Mix coconut yogurt with chia seeds, psyllium husks, and hemp seeds, and leave to swell. In the meantime, clean the strawberries and wash the blueberries. Halve the strawberries. Divide the yogurt and seed mixture between 2 bowls, add the coconut flakes and garnish with the fresh fruit. Cocoa nibs and nuts also go well with this.

2.48 Fruity cabbage salad with blueberries

Preparation: 30 min **Calories:** 111 **Servings:** 4

Ingredients

- 500g red cabbage (0.25 red cabbage)
- iodized salt with fluoride
- 1 sour apple
- 250g blueberries
- 2 tbsp apple cider vinegar
- 2 tbsp lemon juice
- 4 tbsp apple juice
- 1 tbsp maple syrup
- pepper
- 1 tbsp rapeseed oil

Instructions. Cut the apple into wedges. Cut the apple into wedges. How best to sort and wash blueberries How best to sort and wash blueberries. **Preparation.** Wash the cabbage, remove the stalk, finely grate the cabbage, mix with 1 teaspoon of salt and mix well. Let stand for 15-20 minutes, stirring frequently. Meanwhile, wash, quarter, core, and thinly slice the apples. Wash the berries carefully and pat dry. Mix the vinegar, lemon juice, apple juice, maple syrup, pepper, and oil for the vinaigrette. Mix the red cabbage with the vinaigrette, apple, and berries, and season with salt and pepper. Then pour into 4 glasses.

2.49 Turmeric Latte
Preparation: 10 min **Servings:** 1
Ingredients
- 250 ml of coconut milk
- 2 teaspoons of turmeric
- 3 teaspoons of honey
- 10 peppercorns
- the seeds of half a vanilla pod
- cinnamon

Instructions. Prepare all the ingredients you will need for the golden milk. Dilute the coconut milk with half a glass of warm water. Combine all the ingredients in a blender: diluted coconut milk, turmeric, honey, vanilla seeds, and ground pepper. Blend until you have obtained a well-homogeneous and a little frothy mixture. Complete your golden milk with a sprinkle of cinnamon, and serve it garnished with a whole cinnamon stick. As an alternative to cinnamon, you can use star anise, blending it with all the ingredients and leaving it whole on top to decorate.

2.50 Anti-inflammatory porridge
Working time: 5 mins **Completed in:** 10 mins **Calories:** 353 **Servings:** 2
Ingredients
- Oatmeal 60 grams
- Oat bran 1 teaspoon / 3g
- Natural oat milk 250 milliliters
- Apple 1 piece / 250g
- Cinammon 1 teaspoon / 1g

- Maple syrup 1 teaspoon / 8g
- Rosehip powder 1 tablespoon / 10g
- Sunflower seeds 1 tablespoon / 15g
- Hemp oil 2 teaspoons / 12g

Instructions. Bring the oat milk and bran to a boil in a small saucepan. Wash, core, and dice the apple. Once the oat milk is boiling, reduce the heat and stir in the oatmeal. Add apple pieces, cinnamon, and maple syrup, and mix. Simmer on low heat for about 5 minutes, stirring now and then. Finally, stir in the rosehip powder and hemp oil and divide the anti-inflammatory porridge between two bowls. Sprinkle with sunflower seeds and enjoy additional fruit, nuts, or seeds if desired.

2.51 Banana Bread Pecan Overnight Oats

Preparation time: 20 Minutes **Cooking time:** 0 Minutes **Serving:** 5 Persons

Ingredients

- 1 cup old-fashioned rolled oats
- 1 1/2 cups milk
- 1/4 cup Greek yogurt (plain)
- 2 tablespoons honey
- 2 bananas (very ripe, mashed)
- 2 tablespoons coconut flakes
- 1/4 teaspoon sea salt (flaked)
- 1 tablespoon chia seeds
- 2 teaspoons vanilla extract

Topping:

- Banana slices
- Roasted pecans
- Honey
- Pomegranate seeds
- Fig halves

Instructions. To prepare, combine the oats, coconut flakes, bananas, milk, yogurt, honey, chia seeds, vanilla, and sea salt essence in a large mixing dish. Blend together well. Place the oat mixture into two bowls and divide it in half. Cover. The recommended minimum time in the fridge is 6 hours, but overnight is best. Toss the ingredients together and stir. Add the toppings to each plate of oats and serve. Serve.

Nutrition Calories: 370 Kcal, Proteins: 16g, Fat: 8g, Carbohydrates: 58g

2.52 Cinnamon Granola with Fruits

Preparation time: 15 Minutes **Cooking time:** 0 Minutes **Serving:** 5 Persons

Ingredients

- 1/4 cup walnuts (chopped)
- 2 cups old-fashioned rolled oats
- 1/4 cup shredded coconut (unsweetened)
- 1/4 cup dried apricots (chopped)
- 1/4 cup honey
- 1/4 cup raisins
- 4 tablespoons unsalted butter (melted)
- 1/4 teaspoon ground cloves
- 1/4 cup dried cranberries
- 2 tablespoons pumpkin seeds
- 1/4 teaspoon ground nutmeg
- 1/2 teaspoon ground cinnamon

Instructions. Turn the oven temperature up to three hundred degrees F. To prepare a baking sheet, line it with parchment paper. Combine the oats, pumpkin seeds, spices, coconuts, walnuts, and salt in a large mixing basin. Don't bother with it right now. Throw the honey and butter into a separate bowl. Combo together successfully. Add the liquid to the oats and stir. Combo together successfully. Put the oat mix on the prepared baking sheet. The spread was uniform. Put in the oven and bake for 20-25 minutes. Let it cool down a little. Prepare the granola by breaking it up. Combine the granola pieces and dried fruit. Put away in a container with a tight lid.

Nutrition Calories: 120 Kcal, Proteins: 2g, Fat: 4.5g, Carbohydrates: 18g

2.53 Yogurt Parfait with Chia Seeds and Raspberries

Preparation time: 20 Minutes **Cooking time:** 0 Minutes **Serving:** 5 Persons

Ingredients

- 16 ounces yogurt (plain, divided into 4 portions)
- 1/2 cup raspberries (fresh)
- 2 tablespoons chia seeds
- 1 teaspoon maple syrup
- Pinch of cinnamon

Topping:

- Nectarines (sliced)
- Strawberries (sliced)

- Blackberries (sliced)

Instructions. Place the raspberries in a large basin. Combine them and mash them till they resemble jam. Mix with some cinnamon and honey with some chia seeds. Put everything in a blender and blitz it until it's a uniform consistency. Divide into halves and set aside. Put two in the glass. Spread some yogurt on the bottom of each cup. The raspberry filling comes next. The last layer consists of any leftover yogurt. Incorporate the condiments. Serve. **Nutrition** Calories: 252 Kcal, Proteins: 13g, Fat: 12g, Carbohydrates: 25g

2.54 Avocado Toast with Egg
Preparation time: 15 Minutes **Cooking time:** 10 Minutes **Serving:** 4 Persons

Ingredients

- 1 slice of gluten-free bread (toasted)
- 1 1/2 teaspoon ghee
- 1 egg (scrambled)
- Red pepper flakes
- 1/2 avocado (sliced)
- A handful of spinach leaves

Instructions. Apply some ghee to the hot toast. Layer the toast with avocado slices. Spinach leaves are a great garnish. The scrambled egg should be served on top. Add some crushed red pepper for heat. **Nutrition** Calories: 260 Kcal, Proteins: 12g, Fat: 16g, Carbohydrates: 20g

2.55 Winter Morning Breakfast Bowl
Preparation time: 15 Minutes **Cooking time:** 0 Minutes **Serving:** 4 Persons

Ingredients

- 1 cup of quinoa
- 2 1/2 cups coconut water
- 2 whole cloves
- 1-star anise pod
- 1 cinnamon stick

Fresh Fruits:

- Blackberries
- Apples
- Cranberries
- Persimmons
- Pears

Instructions. Put the coconut water, quinoa, and seasonings into a pot and cook it over medium heat. Simmer them until they reach a rolling boil. Put the lid on it. Turn down the stove.

The recommended cooking time is 25 minutes. Split the quinoa in half and place it in separate dishes. Do not use entire spices. Put some fruit on top of each dish. Serve.

Nutrition Calories: 257 Kcal, Proteins: 12g, Fat: 8g, Carbohydrates: 40g

2.56 Scrambled Tofu Breakfast Tacos

Preparation time: 5 Minutes **Cooking time:** 10 Minutes **Serving:** 4 Persons

Ingredients

- 1/2 cup grape tomatoes, quartered
- 12 ounces tofu, pressed, drained
- 1 medium red pepper, diced
- 1 clove of garlic, minced
- 8 corn tortillas
- 1 medium avocado, sliced
- 1/4 teaspoon ground turmeric
- 1 teaspoon olive oil
- 1/4 teaspoon salt
- 1/4 teaspoon ground black pepper
- 1/4 teaspoon cumin

Instructions. Put the oil in a skillet and heat it over a moderate flame; when the oil is heated, add the garlic and pepper and sauté for Two minutes. Crumble in some tofu, season it with salt, black pepper, and all the seasonings, and cook it for 5 minutes while stirring occasionally. When ready, divide the tofu among the tortillas, then top with the tomato and avocado.

Nutrition Calories: 240 Kcal, Proteins: 12g, Fat: 8g, Carbohydrates: 26g

2.57 Potato Skillet Breakfast

Preparation time: 5 Minutes **Cooking time:** 15 Minutes **Serving:** 5 Persons

Ingredients

- 1 1/4 pounds potatoes, diced
- 1 ½ cup cooked black beans
- 12 ounces spinach
- 2 small avocados, sliced, for topping
- 1 1/4 pounds red potatoes, diced
- 1 medium green bell pepper, diced
- 1 large white onion, diced
- 1 jalapeno, minced

- 1 medium red bell pepper, diced

- 1/2 teaspoon red chili powder

- 3 cloves of garlic, minced

- 1/4 teaspoon salt

- 1 tablespoon canola oil

- 1 teaspoon cumin

Instructions. A preheated oven is ready in a short amount of time, so turn it on and set the temperature to 425 degrees F. Secondly, heat the oil in a skillet over moderate heat. When the oil is heated, add the potatoes and cook, often stirring, for 2 minutes before seasoning with salt, chili powder, and cumin. Put the pan in the microwave and bake the potatoes for twenty minutes, tossing once halfway through until they are done. After 15 minutes, add the rest of the onion, garlic, bell peppers, and jalapeño and continue roasting, turning once halfway through. Place skillet over moderate heat and cook for 5-10 minutes, occasionally stirring, until potatoes are tender. Add beans and spinach and simmer for another 3 minutes, occasionally stirring, till basil leaves have wilted. When finished, sprinkle the pan with chopped cilantro and serve with avocado.

Nutrition Calories: 199 Kcal, Proteins: 4g, Fat: 7g, Carbohydrates: 32g

2.58 Peanut Butter and Banana Bread Granola
Preparation time: 10 Minutes **Cooking time:** 32 Minutes **Serving:** 6 Persons

Ingredients

- 1/2 cup mashed banana

- 1/2 cup Quinoa

- 3 cup rolled oats, old-fashioned

- 1 cup peanuts, salted

- 1 cup banana chips, crushed

- 1 teaspoon. salt

- 1/4 cup brown sugar

- 1 teaspoon. cinnamon

- 1/4 cup honey

- 1/3 cup peanut butter

- 2 teaspoons. vanilla extract, unsweetened

- 6 tablespoons. unsalted butter

Instructions. Turn on the microwave and prepare it for 325 degrees Fahrenheit. Prepare two lined baking trays ahead of time by lining them with parchment paper and setting them away. Stir together the oats, banana chips, quinoa, cinnamon, sugar, and salt in a bowl. Put the butter and nectar in a small pan and heat them over low flame, often stirring, for about 4 minutes, or till the honey has melted. Then, take the pan off the heat and toss in the banana and vanilla until well combined. Finally, add this to the grain mixture and mix to combine. Cook the granola for 20-25 minutes, until golden brown, dividing the mixture equally between two baking pans. Cool the granola completely on the baking sheets set over wire racks before breaking it up and serving. As soon as possible, serve.

Nutrition Calories: 655 Kcal, Proteins: 18g, Fat: 36g, Carbohydrates: 70g

2.59 Chocolate Chip, Strawberry and Oat Waffles
Preparation time: 10 Minutes **Cooking time:** 25 Minutes **Serving:** 6 Persons

Ingredients

- 6 tablespoons chocolate chips, semi-sweet
- 1/4 teaspoon salt
- ½ cup chopped strawberries
- 2 teaspoons baking powder

Wet Ingredients:

- 1/3 cup mashed bananas
- Powdered sugar as needed for topping

Dry Ingredients:

- 1/4 cup oats
- 2 tablespoon maple syrup
- 2 tablespoon coconut oil
- 1/2 teaspoon vanilla extract, unsweetened
- 1 1/2 tablespoon ground flaxseeds
- 1 1/2 cup whole wheat pastry flour
- 2 1/2 tablespoon cocoa powder
- 1/4 cup applesauce, unsweetened
- 1 3/4 cup almond milk, unsweetened

Instructions. Put the dry components in a medium bowl and whisk them together. Put the liquid components in a medium bowl and mix until blended. Add the dry ingredients and whisk in four separate batches just until combined. In the meanwhile, turn on the griddle and let it heat up to a high temperature while you let the batter sit out at ambient temperature for Five minutes.

Then, spoon in a sixth of the mixture and bake until the pancake is firm and golden. Keep making waffles in a similar fashion until all the batter is gone, then sprinkle the finished waffles with sugar and top with cocoa powder and fruit.

Nutrition Calories: 261 Kcal, Proteins: 6g, Fat: 10g, Carbohydrates: 41g

2.60 Chickpea Flour Omelet

Preparation time: 5 Minutes **Cooking time:** 12 Minutes **Serving:** 1 Person

Ingredients

- Approximately one-half of a teaspoon of chopped chives
- 1/4 cup of chickpea flour
- 1/2 cup of chopped spinach
- 1/4 tsp. of garlic powder
- Exactly a Cup and a Tablespoon of Water
- A pinch of turmeric
- Black pepper, ground, 1/8 teaspoon
- 1/2 teaspoon of yeast extract
- The equivalent of half a teaspoon of baking powder
- 1/2 tsp. egg substitute for vegans

Instructions. Put everything, save from the spinach, in a bowl and whisk to incorporate. Set aside for 5 minutes. Then, heat some oil in a skillet and set it over low heat. When the pan is heated, add the ingredients and let them cook for three minutes or until the edges are dry. Then place spinach over half of the omelet, fold over the other half, and cook for 2 minutes more. The omelet should be slid onto a platter and served with ketchup.

Nutrition Calories: 151 Kcal, Proteins: 10g, Fat: 2g, Carbohydrates: 24g

CHAPTER 3: Anti-Inflammatory Lunch Recipes

3.1 Buddha Bowl with Avocado, Wild Rice, Kale, and Orange
Preparation time: 15 Minutes **Cooking time:** 12 Minutes **Serving:** 4 Persons

Ingredients

Rice:

- 1 cup wild rice
- 3 cups vegetable broth
- 1 garlic clove (minced)
- 2 tablespoons extra-virgin olive oil
- 2 tablespoons rice vinegar
- 1 tablespoon fresh mint (chopped)
- Salt
- Freshly ground black pepper

Toppings:

- 1/4 cup pumpkin seeds
- 1/4 cup pomegranate seeds
- 1 bunch kale (roughly chopped)
- Salt
- 1 orange (segmented)
- 2 eggs (hard-boiled)
- 1/2 avocado (sliced)
- 2 tablespoons olive oil
- 1 tablespoon rice vinegar
- Freshly ground black pepper

Instructions. Rice: Put the broth, garlic, and rice in a saucepan and simmer it over medium heat. Combine ingredients by stirring. Get it boiling. Turn down the stove. Allow the rice to simmer for fifteen min or until cooked, and all liquid has been absorbed. Wait 10 minutes before serving so the rice can cool down. Mint, olive oil, vinegar, salt, and pepper should be added. Mix thoroughly with the rice by tossing. **Toppings:** Combine the kale, olive oil, and vinegar in a large bowl. Blend together by giving it a good toss. Divide the rice in half and put it in two separate dishes. Sprinkle the kale mixture over the rice in each dish. Spread the remaining condiments across the two serving dishes evenly. Add some salt and pepper for flavor. Serve.

Nutrition Calories: 1059 Kcal, Proteins: 65g, Fat: 38g, Carbohydrates: 108g

3.2 Avocado Chickpea Salad Sandwich

Preparation time: 12 Minutes **Cooking time:** 15 Minutes **Serving:** 6 Persons

Ingredients

- 1 15-ounce-can chickpea (drained and rinsed)
- 1 large avocado (ripe)
- Freshly ground pepper
- 2 teaspoons lime juice
- 1/4 cup cranberries (dried)
- 4 slices of whole grain bread
- Salt

Toppings:

- Arugula
- Red onion
- Spinach

Instructions. Put the chickpeas in a big basin and stir them around. Use a fork to mix them up. Prepare the avocado by placing it inside. Keep crushing it until it's mostly fine with some lumpy bits. Cranberries and fresh lemon juice should be added. Add some salt and pepper for flavor. Combine in a harmonious manner. The bread should be toasted. The chickpea mixture should be divided in half. Spread one serving onto a piece of toast. Apply your preferred toppings on the top. Add another piece of bread to finish the sandwich. Serve.

Nutrition Calories: 340 Kcal, Proteins: 15g, Fat: 12g, Carbohydrates: 46g

3.3 Spiced Lentil Soup

Preparation time: 20 Minutes **Cooking time:** 20 Minutes **Serving:** 4 Persons

Ingredients

- 3/4 cup red lentils (rinsed, uncooked, and drained)
- 3 1/2 cups vegetable broth (low-sodium)
- 1 1/2 tablespoons extra-virgin olive oil
- 1 large onion (diced)
- 2 garlic cloves (minced)
- Freshly ground black pepper
- 1 14-ounce-can coconut milk (full-fat)
- 1 5-ounce-package baby spinach
- 1 14-ounce-can diced tomatoes (with juice)
- 2 teaspoons turmeric (ground)

- 1 1/2 teaspoons cumin (ground)
- 2 teaspoons fresh lime juice
- 1/2 teaspoon fine sea salt
- 1/4 teaspoon cardamom (ground)
- 1/2 teaspoon cinnamon
- Cayenne pepper

Instructions Put the oil into a pan and heat it over medium heat. To soften the onion, sauté it with garlic and salt. Cardamom, turmeric, cumin, and cinnamon should be added now. Combine ingredients by stirring. Continue cooking for one minute. Mix in the red lentils, broth, cayenne pepper, black pepper, coconut milk, and salt. Mix well by stirring. Let the liquid reach a rolling boil. Turn down the stove. Allow the ingredients to boil for twenty minutes. Soft and airy le nails are ideal. Take it away from the stove. Do not forget the spinach! Combine ingredients by stirring. Add some salt, pepper, and lime juice for seasoning. Serve.

Nutrition Calories: 331 Kcal, Proteins: 30g, Fat: 3.6g, Carbohydrates: 47.5g

3.4 Red Lentil Pasta with Tomato

Preparation time: 15 Minutes **Cooking time:** 10 Minutes **Serving:** 4 Persons

Ingredients

- 1/4 cup extra virgin olive oil
- 1/2 cup sun-dried tomatoes (oil-packed, drained, and chopped)
- 6 cloves garlic (minced)
- 2 large handfuls of kale
- 1 sweet onion (chopped)
- 1 can (28 ounces) fire roasted tomatoes
- 1 tablespoon oregano (dried)
- 1 box (8 ounces) of red lentil pasta
- 1 tablespoon basil (dried)
- 2 teaspoons turmeric (ground)
- 1 tablespoon apple cider vinegar
- Pepper
- Toasted pine nuts (for topping)
- Kosher salt

Instructions. Put the oil into a pan and heat it over medium heat. The onion should be sautéed for 5 minutes or until tender. Garlic, basil, oregano, turmeric, salt, and pepper should be stirred in. Continue cooking for one minute. Roasted tomatoes, please (juice included). Stir the tomatoes until they are crushed. Add the solar tomatoes and balsamic vinegar.

Put the pot on low heat and simmer for fifteen min. Toss the greens in and mix it up. 5 additional minutes of cooking time are required. The red lentil spaghetti should be prepared as directed on the box. Divide the spaghetti into 6 bowls into equal amounts. Sprinkle some pine nuts and tomato sauce on top of each bowl. Serve.

Nutrition Calories: 270 Kcal, Proteins: 8.5g, Fat: 4.5g, Carbohydrates: 49g

3.5 Tuna Mediterranean Salad
Preparation time: 15 Minutes **Cooking time:** 05 Minutes **Serving:** 4 Persons

Ingredients

- 1 14.5-ounce-can chickpea (drained and rinsed)
- 2 cans Albacore Tuna (drained)
- 1 cup red peppers (roasted and chopped)
- 1/2 cup pepperocini (diced)
- 1/3 cup parsley (finely chopped)
- 1/4 cup feta cheese
- 1 cucumber (chopped)
- 1/2 red onion (diced)
- 2 teaspoons capers
- Pinch of fine sea salt
- Sundried tomatoes (chopped)
- Olives
- Pinch of black pepper

Dressing:

- 2 tablespoons olive oil
- Pinch black pepper
- 2 tablespoons red wine vinegar
- 1 teaspoon lemon juice
- Pinch fine salt
- 1 teaspoon dried parsley
- 1 teaspoon dried oregano

Instructions. Put everything for the salad into a large mixing basin. Throw everything for the dressing into a separate dish. Stir the whisk vigorously. Coat the salad with the dressing. Throw everything together in a bowl and toss. Serve with half of an avocado.

Nutrition Calories: 230 Kcal, Proteins: 28g, Fat: 10g, Carbohydrates: 40g

3.6 Chicken and Greek Salad Wrap

Preparation time: 15 Minutes **Cooking time:** 25 Minutes **Serving:** 2 Persons

Ingredients

- 1 tablespoon olive oil (divided)
- 2 chicken breasts (bone-in)
- 1/2 teaspoon dried oregano
- 1/2 teaspoon lemon pepper
- 1/2 teaspoon garlic powder

Salad:

- 1/3 cup feta cheese
- 4 cups romaine (chopped)
- 1/3 cup cherry tomatoes (sliced)
- 1/4 cup red onion
- red wine vinegar
- 1/2 cup cucumber slices (chopped)
- 4 tablespoons hummus
- 1/2 teaspoon dried oregano
- 2 tablespoons kalamata olives
- 2 gluten-free wraps
- olive oil
- 1 fresh lemon wedge (juiced)

Instructions. Salad: Put the romaine, cucumbers, tomatoes, onion, oregano, cheese, and olives in a bowl and toss. Use duality of the vinegar, one twist of the canola oil, and the juice of half a lemon to dress the salad. Mix by tossing. **Chicken:** Bake at 375 degrees Fahrenheit, which requires preheating the oven. Prepare a foil-lined baking sheet. Use a drizzle of olive oil, around half of the whole amount. The chicken should be placed on the prepared baking sheet. Add some salt, pepper, pepper flakes, garlic powder, oregano, and lemon pepper for flavor. Using the remaining olive oil, drizzle the mixture. Bake at 400 degrees for 40 minutes. Completely chill the chicken before serving. Cut into manageable chunks. **Wrap:** Smear each wrap with 2 tablespoons of hummus. Add the salad and chicken pieces in layers. Wrap. Serve.

Nutrition Calories: 230 Kcal, Proteins: 39g, Fat: 28g, Carbohydrates: 22g

3.7 Cauliflower and Chickpea Coconut Curry

Preparation time: 15 Minutes **Cooking time:** 25 Minutes **Serving:** 2 Persons

Ingredients

- 1 can (14 ounces) of coconut milk

- 1 can (28 ounces) of cooked chickpeas
- 1/4 cup fresh cilantro (chopped)
- 1 1/2 cups frozen peas
- 4 scallions (thinly sliced)
- 1 red onion (thinly sliced)
- 1 red bell pepper (thinly sliced)
- 1 lime (halved)
- 3 garlic cloves (minced)
- 1 small head cauliflower (bite-size florets)
- 3 tablespoons red curry paste
- 1 tablespoon extra-virgin olive oil
- Salt
- 1 tablespoon fresh ginger (minced)
- 1 teaspoon ground coriander
- Freshly ground black pepper
- 2 teaspoons chili powder

Instructions. Put the oil into a pan and heat it over medium heat. For 5 minutes, sauté the bell pepper and onion. Place the ginger and garlic in the dish. Add another minute to the sautéing. Include coriander, cauliflower, curry paste, and chili powder. Prepare for one minute. Add the coconut milk and heat through. Stir. When the cauliflower is soft, remove it from the fire and discard the bay leaf. Lime juice should be added to the curry. Stir. Include the chickpeas and peas. Add some salt and pepper for flavor. Just let it a few minutes to boil. Sprinkle a spoonful of scallions and parsley over each serving. Serve.

Nutrition Calories: 442 Kcal, Proteins: 15g, Fat: 12g, Carbohydrates: 33g

3.8 Butternut Squash Carrot Soup
Preparation time: 20 Minutes **Cooking time:** 15 Minutes **Serving:** 4 Persons

Ingredients

- 1 pound of carrots (chopped)
- 1 1/2 pounds of butternut squash (peeled and chopped)
- 4 cups vegetable stock
- 1 can coconut milk (full-fat)
- 1/2 cup shallots (sliced)
- 1 teaspoon salt
- 2 tablespoons avocado oil
- Freshly ground black pepper

- 1 tablespoon fresh ginger (grated)

Garnishing:

- Roasted chickpeas
- Coconut milk
- Cilantro

Instructions. Turn the oven temperature up to 400 degrees F. Spread parchment paper on a baking pan. Scatter the carrots, butternut squash, and shallots on the prepared baking sheet. Add oil and drizzle. Add some salt. Give the veggies a little toss to coat. Put them in the oven for 30 minutes at 375 degrees. Give them a few minutes to calm off. Combine the roasted veggies, vegetable stock, coconut milk, ginger, salt, and pepper in a blender. Creamy consistency may be achieved by blending. Put some soup in each of the four bowls. Top each serving with chickpeas, coconut milk, and cilantro.

Nutrition Calories: 129 Kcal, Proteins: 6.5g, Fat: 2.7g, Carbohydrates: 23g

3.9 Kale Quinoa Shrimp Bowl

Preparation time: 25 Minutes **Cooking time:** 30 Minutes **Serving:** 4 Persons

Ingredients

Quinoa:

- 1 1/4 cups quinoa
- 2 cups chicken broth
- Salt
- 2 teaspoons extra-virgin olive oil
- Freshly ground pepper

Kale:

- 2 tablespoons extra-virgin olive oil
- Salt
- 1 bunch lacinato kale (roughly torn)
- Freshly ground black pepper

Shrimp and Toppings:

- 2 watermelon radishes (thinly sliced)
- 1 pound shrimp (peeled and deveined)
- 2 avocados (sliced)
- 1 tablespoon extra-virgin olive oil
- 2 tablespoons hot sauce
- 3/4 teaspoon ground coriander
- Salt

- Freshly ground black pepper
- 1 teaspoon ground cumin

Instructions. Quinoa: Put the olive oil in a saucepan and heat it over medium heat. Combine in the quinoa and mix well. Toasted for one minute. Add to the stock. The quinoa has to boil until it is cooked. Add some salt and pepper for flavor. **Kale:** Turn the oven temperature up to 400 degrees F. Use parchment paper to line a baking sheet. Blend the olive oil and kale together in a large mixing bowl. Add some salt and pepper for flavor. Mix by tossing. Toss the kale with the olive oil and spread it out in a thin layer on the baking sheet. For extra-crispy results, roast for fifteen minutes. **Shrimp and Toppings:** Olive oil should be heated in a pan over medium heat. Toss the shrimp with the cumin, coriander, spicy sauce, salt, and pepper in a mixing dish. Mix by tossing. Heat a pan over medium-high heat and sauté the shrimp mixture for 5 minutes. Distribute the quinoa among four serving dishes. Crispy kale, avocado slices, watermelon radishes, and shrimp provide a delicious topping for the soup. Serve.

Nutrition Calories: 377 Kcal, Proteins: 37g, Fat: 7g, Carbohydrates: 436g

3.10 Egg Bowl and Veggies
Preparation time: 15 Minutes **Cooking time:** 05 Minutes **Serving:** 4 Persons

Ingredients

- 1 pound Brussels sprouts (cut in half)
- 1 pound sweet potatoes (diced)
- 4 eggs (poached)
- 1 1/2 tablespoons olive oil
- 3 tablespoons apple cider vinegar
- 2 cups arugula
- 2 tablespoons harissa

Instructions. Turn on the oven and set the temperature to 450 degrees F. Use parchment paper to line a baking sheet. Sprinkle the Brussels sprouts and sweet potatoes evenly over the prepared baking sheet. Swirl in some olive oil. Add some salt and pepper for flavor. Cook at 400°F for 20 minutes, or until meat is tender. Combine the harissa, olive oil, and apple cider vinegar in a separate bowl. Divvy up the roasted veggies into 4 serving dishes. Scatter arugula, harissa, and an egg dressing on each bowl. Serve.

Nutrition Calories: 263 Kcal, Proteins: 16g, Fat: 20g, Carbohydrates: 4.6g

3.11 Turkey Taco Bowls
Preparation time: 20 Minutes **Cooking time:** 15 Minutes **Serving:** 2 Persons

Ingredients

Turkey:

- 2/3 cup water
- 3/4 pound ground turkey (lean)

- 2 tablespoons taco seasoning

Salsa:

- 1/4 cup red onion (finely chopped)
- 1-pint cherry tomatoes (halved)
- 1 jalapeno (finely chopped)
- 1/2 lime (juiced)
- 1/8 teaspoon salt

Rice:

- 3/4 cup brown rice (uncooked)
- 1/8 teaspoon salt
- 1 lime (zested)

Topping:

- 1 can (12 ounces) of corn kernels (drained)
- 1/2 cup mozzarella (shredded)

Instructions. Follow the package directions for cooking the brown rice. It's as simple as seasoning the boiling water with salt and lime zest. Put the hot rice in a separate bowl to cool down. Put the turkey into a skillet and cook it over medium heat. Leave the turkey in the oven for 10 minutes, or until it's no pinker inside. Add the water and taco seasoning to the pot. Combine ingredients by stirring. Keep the pot on low heat for two min to smooth the sauce. Put the turkey in a bowl of ice water. Put all the salsa ingredients into a large mixing bowl. Throw everything together in a bowl and toss. Divide the rice among 4 serving dishes. Turkey and salsa may be used as toppings for the rice bowls. Scatter the corn kernels and mozzarella over the top. Serve.

Nutrition Calories: 580 Kcal, Proteins: 26g, Fat: 25g, Carbohydrates: 62g

3.12 Bulgur Kale Pesto Salad

Preparation time: 10 Minutes **Cooking time:** 05 Minutes **Serving:** 2 Persons

Ingredients

- 1 1/2 cups bulgur
- 1/2 pound of green beans
- 1/2 cup packed basil leaves
- 1/4 cup plus 3 tablespoons almonds (toasted)
- 1 cup lacinato kale (thinly sliced)
- 1/4 cup lemon juice
- 1-pint grape tomatoes (halved)
- 1/4 cup extra-virgin olive oil

- 1/4 packed flat-leaf parsley

- 3 tablespoons almonds (sliced)

- 1 garlic clove

- 1 teaspoon kosher salt (divided)

- 1/2 teaspoon kosher salt

- 1/4 teaspoon ground black pepper

Instructions. Place the garlic cloves in the bowl of a food processor. Chop it up in the food processor. Add the almonds, basil, parsley, and kale. Pulse it until it's finely chopped. Add the lime juice, pepper, and a half teaspoon of salt. Blend everything up until it's silky smooth. Pesto is poured into bulgur. Incorporate the leftover toasted almonds, the green beans, and the tomatoes. Toss. Sprinkle some sliced almonds on top. Serve.

Nutrition Calories: 218 Kcal, Proteins: 5.6g, Fat: 14g, Carbohydrates: 18g

3.13 Turkish Scrambled Eggs

Preparation time: 08 Minutes **Cooking time:** 05 Minutes **Serving:** 4 Persons

Ingredients

- 4 ripe tomatoes (diced)

- 6 eggs (beaten)

- 4 whole grain pitas (serving)

- 2 tablespoons olive oil

- 3 scallions (finely chopped)

- Green olives (garnish)

- 2 tablespoons fresh parsley (chopped)

- 4 ounces Feta cheese (crumbled)

- 2 large red bell peppers (seeded and finely chopped)

- 1 teaspoon red pepper flakes (crushed)

- 1/4 teaspoon ground black pepper

- 1/2 teaspoon kosher salt

Instructions. The oil should be heated in a pan on moderate heat. The scallions need two minutes of cooking time to soften in the pan. Place the peppers inside. Stir-fry for five minutes. The tomatoes and pepper flakes should be added now. Add another five minutes of sautéing. Toss in some eggs and cheese. Shake and mix incessantly to create a scramble. The eggs need to be cooked through. Add some salt and pepper for flavor. Remove the heat source. Include the chopped parsley in the mixture. Spread olives on top. Pitas should be served on the side.

Nutrition Calories: 240 Kcal, Proteins: 12g, Fat: 14g, Carbohydrates: 19g

3.14 Swiss Chard and Red Lentil Curried Soup

Preparation time: 18 Minutes **Cooking time:** 10 Minutes **Serving:** 4 Persons

Ingredients

- 2 cups dried red lentils
- 1 pound Swiss chard
- 5 cups vegetable broth
- 6 tablespoons thick Greek yogurt
- 1 can (15 ounces) of chickpeas (rinsed and drained)
- 5 teaspoons curry powder
- 1 large onion (thinly sliced)
- 2 tablespoons olive oil
- 1 lime (sliced into 6 wedges)
- 1/4 teaspoon ground cayenne pepper
- 1 red jalapeño chili (stemmed and thinly sliced)
- 1 teaspoon salt

Instructions. Put the oil in a pot and heat it over medium heat. When the onion is soft and translucent, it's ready to be sautéed. Curry and cayenne pepper should be stirred in. Place the chard and Four cups of broth into the pot. Keep stirring at a boil till the chard is wilted, about 5 minutes. Add the lentils and chickpeas and stir. Turn down the stove. Stir occasionally and cook at a low simmer for 18 minutes or until lentils are tender. Get rid of the hot water or the heater. About ½ of the soup should be put in a food processor. Into a smooth consistency, of course. Return the puréed mixture to the cooking kettle. Add the remaining salt and broth. Stir. Get the soup nice and toasty for a few minutes on low heat. Distribute across 6 bowls. Yogurt, a lime wedge, and sliced jalapenos make a great garnish. Serve.

Nutrition Calories: 169 Kcal, Proteins: 10g, Fat: 2.82g, Carbohydrates: 26g

3.15 Orange Cardamom Quinoa with Carrots

Preparation time: 15 Minutes **Cooking time:** 0 Minutes **Serving:** 4 Persons

Ingredients

- 2 1/2 cups vegetable broth
- 1 pound of carrots (peeled and sliced)
- 1 cup quinoa (rinsed)
- 2 oranges (zested and segmented)
- 1/3 cup golden raisins
- 1-inch fresh ginger (peeled and minced)
- 1 teaspoon ground cardamom

- 1/2 teaspoon freshly ground black pepper
- 1/2 teaspoon salt

Instructions. The orange zest, salt, black pepper, cardamom, raisins, ginger, carrots, quinoa, and broth go into the slow cooker. Combo together successfully. For a low and slow cooking time of 3 1/2 hours, start this. Evenly disperse the quinoa between 4 serving dishes. Add a few orange segments on the top of each serving. Serve.

Nutrition Calories: 170 Kcal, Proteins: 5g, Fat: 3g, Carbohydrates: 31g

3.16 Quinoa Turmeric Power Bowl

Preparation time: 15 Minutes **Cooking time:** 30 Minutes **Serving:** 4 Persons

Ingredients

- 2 kale leaves (rinsed)
- 7 small yellow potatoes (slice into strips)
- 1 avocado (sliced)
- 1 can (15 ounces) of chickpeas (drained and rinsed)
- Pepper
- 1/4 cup quinoa
- 1 tablespoon coconut oil
- 1 teaspoon paprika
- Salt
- 1/2 tablespoon olive oil
- 2 teaspoons turmeric(divided)

Instructions. Turn the oven temperature up to 360 degrees Fahrenheit. Place the potato strips flat on half of the baking sheet. Coconut oil should be drizzled over the top. Add some salt, pepper, and turmeric (about a teaspoon's worth) for seasoning. Keep turning after 5 minutes. Put the paprika and chickpeas in a large bowl and mix well. Blend well by tossing. On the opposite side of the baking sheet, separate the chickpeas from the potatoes. Toss in the oven and set the timer for 25 minutes. Put half a cup of liquid and the quinoa in a saucepan and cook it on low to medium heat. Let the quinoa simmer until it's soft. Spice it up with a pinch of turmeric, some pepper, and salt. Blend well. Putting it aside to cool is a good idea. The kale benefits from a massage with olive oil. Split the leaves between 4 serving dishes. Arrange quinoa, avocado slices, and roasted veggies in separate bowls. Serve.

Nutrition Calories: 470 Kcal, Proteins: 14g, Fat: 17g, Carbohydrates: 72g

3.17 Tomato Stew with Chickpea and Kale

Preparation time: 15 Minutes **Cooking time:** 20 Minutes **Serving:** 4 Persons

Ingredients

- 3/4 pound kale (stemmed and leaves coarsely chopped)

- 1 pound of tomatoes (cored and chopped)
- 1 cup vegetable stock
- 1 medium onion (sliced into eighths)
- 2 cans (15-ounce) chickpeas (drained and rinsed)
- 6 garlic cloves (thinly sliced)
- 1/4 teaspoon red pepper flakes (crushed)
- 4 tablespoons olive oil (divided)
- 4 large eggs
- 1 1/4 teaspoon kosher salt (divided)

Instructions. A quarter of the oil should be heated in a pan on moderate heat. Coupling the onion with a quarter of the salt is the first step. In a skillet, heat the oil and cook the onions for 10 mins. Add the crushed red pepper and minced garlic and stir. Keep cooking for another two minutes. Include the kale. Get it as soft as possible by cooking it. Add the canned tomatoes, chickpeas, and chicken stock. Prepare in ten minutes. Just add salt. Put the remaining oil in a pan and heat it over medium heat. Prepare an egg by cracking it open and cooking it till the white is done and the bottom becomes crunchy. Repeat with the remaining eggs. Create 4 bowls and equally distribute the stew. Add an egg on top. Just add salt. Serve.

Nutrition Calories: 212 Kcal, Proteins: 6.4g, Fat: 5.1g, Carbohydrates: 37g

3.18 Anti-Inflammatory Beef Meatballs
Preparation time: 10 Minutes **Cooking time:** 10 Minutes **Serving:** 4 Persons

Ingredients

- 1/4 cup chopped cilantro (tightly packed)
- 2 pounds of ground beef
- 1/2 teaspoon ground ginger
- Zest of 1 lime
- 1/2 teaspoon sea salt
- 5 garlic cloves (pressed)

Instructions. Turn on the oven and set the temperature to 350 degrees F. Put parchment paper on a baking sheet. Put everything you need in a basin and mix it together. Maintain a healthy blend. Make 12 meatballs from the mixture. Line a baking sheet with foil and distribute the meatballs on it. Put it in the oven and set the timer for 25 minutes. You may garnish the meatballs with fresh herbs and avocado slices.

Nutrition Calories: 57 Kcal, Proteins: 4g, Fat: 7g, Carbohydrates: 3g

3.19 Salmon with Veggies Sheet Pan

Preparation time: 20 Minutes **Cooking time:** 30 Minutes **Serving:** 4 Persons

Ingredients

- 16 ounces bag of baby potatoes
- 1 teaspoon fresh thyme
- 16 ounces Brussels sprouts (halved)
- 4 6-ounce salmon fillets (skin on)
- 1 cup cherry tomatoes
- 1/2 red onion (cubed)
- 1 bunch of asparagus (trimmed and halved)
- 3 tablespoons balsamic vinegar
- 1 garlic clove (minced)
- 2 tablespoons honey
- 1 tablespoon Dijon mustard
- 2 tablespoons olive oil
- 1/2 teaspoon sea salt

Instructions. Prepare a 450 F oven temperature. Prepare parchment paper on a baking pan. To make the dressing, combine the vinegar, garlic, honey, Dijon mustard, thyme, and salt in a bowl. Maintain a healthy blend. Asparagus, red onion, Brussels sprouts, potatoes, tomatoes, olive oil, and Three tbsp. The balsamic honey combination should be combined in a separate bowl. Maintain a healthy blend. Prepare a baking sheet by spreading the veggies equally over it. Put in the oven for 10 minutes. The oven is done, so remove it. Salmon fillets should be arranged atop the veggies. It's skin-side down. Apply the remaining balsamic honey mixture to each fillet by brushing it on. The baking sheet should be returned to the oven. Put in the oven for 10 minutes. For the next four minutes, broil on high. The fillets' exposed surfaces will brown in this manner. Serve.

Nutrition Calories: 377 Kcal, Proteins: 38g, Fat: 10g, Carbohydrates: 39g

3.20 Roasted Salmon Garlic and Broccoli

Preparation time: 25 Minutes **Cooking time:** 35 Minutes **Serving:** 4 Persons

Ingredients

- 1 lemon (sliced)
- 1 1/2 pounds salmon fillets
- 1 large broccoli head (sliced into florets)
- 2 1/2 tablespoons coconut oil (melted and divided)
- 3/4 teaspoon sea salt (divided)
- 2 cloves fresh garlic (minced)

- Black pepper

Instructions. Prepare a 450 F oven temperature. Put parchment paper on a baking sheet. Put the salmon in an even layer on the prepared baking sheet. There has to be breathing room between the various components. A teaspoon of olive oil should be used to finish cooking the salmon. Distribute the garlic cloves in a thin layer over the fish. Add ½ of the salt and enough pepper to taste. Place a lemon slice atop each serving of fish. Putting aside. Place the broccoli florets, remaining pepper, salt, and 1 1/2 teaspoons of oil in a mixing basin and toss to combine. Toss. Florets should be placed between each slice of salmon. Put the dish in the oven, and set the timer for fifteen min. Parsley and lemon wedges make a lovely garnish. Serve.

Nutrition Calories: 366 Kcal, Proteins: 35g, Fat: 14g, Carbohydrates: 29g

3.21 Mediterranean Salad with Tuna

Ingredients

For the marinade:
- 2 Umi Foods tuna steaks
- 2 stalks of rosemary
- ½ tbsp oregano
- 1 Lemon
- 1 tablespoon olive oil
- 1 teaspoon salt
- 1 teaspoon garlic powder

For the salad:
- ¼ bunch of basil
- ¼ bunch of spinach
- 30 gr tomate cherry
- 30 g fresh cheese
- 2 pieces of sliced bread
- Olive oil
- 2 lemons
- Salt and pepper to taste

Instructions. We start by marinating the tuna with rosemary, oregano, lemon, salt, garlic powder, and olive oil for at least one hour before preparing the salad. Once the tuna is ready, fry it in vegetable oil over medium heat 3 minutes per side and let it rest. We prepare the salad by cutting the basil and spinach in halves. We cut the fresh cheese into cubes. For the sliced, bread or the one of your choice, we cut it into cubes and put it in the oven at 180°C for 3 to 4 minutes or until it is golden and crispy. We sauté the cherry tomatoes in olive oil with a little salt. We season our salad with olive oil, salt, and pepper to taste the set of 2 lemons.

3.22 Lemon Chicken with Quinoa Pepper Salad

Working time: 35 min **Completed in:** 45 min **Calories:** 553 **Servings:** 2

Ingredients

- Chicken Breast (Organic) 250 grams
- organic lemon 1pc /50g
- quinoa 100 gram
- paprika (yellow) 1 piece / 150g
- paprika (red) 1 piece / 150g
- zucchini/s 1pc /300g
- Chickpeas (jar/can) 100 gram
- olive oil (virgin) 4 tablespoons / 30g
- thyme (dried) some / 1g
- Balsamic vinegar 2 tablespoons / 15g
- Salt 1 teaspoon / 5g
- Pepper some / 1g

Instructions. Grate 1 teaspoon lemon zest and squeeze lemon halves. Rinse the chicken breast fillets, pat dry, place in a freezer bag with the lemon juice and salt and pepper, knead well and marinate in the fridge for at least 20 minutes. Cook quinoa in salted water according to package instructions. Drain the chickpeas, wash the peppers and courgettes, deseed the peppers, and cut both into small pieces (1 to 1.5 cm). Add the chickpeas, peppers, and zucchini to the quinoa for the last 8 minutes and cook. Then let it cool down for at least 10 minutes. Heat the oil in a pan over medium-high, sear the chicken breasts for 5 to 6 minutes on each side, and season with salt, pepper, and thyme. Let cool down. Mix the vegetables, chickpeas, quinoa, thyme, and balsamic vinegar. Thickly slice the lemon chicken, serve with the quinoa salad, and place in a carrier.

3.23 Spinach omelet with pesto

Preparation: 55 min **Calories:** 429 kcal **Servings:** 4

Ingredients

- 20g _ basil (1 bunch)
- 1 clove of garlic
- 30g _ pine nuts (2 tbsp)
- salt
- pepper
- 1 tsp lemon juice
- 7 tbsp olive oil
- 200g _ spinach
- 4 tbsp whipped cream
- 8th eggs
- 20g _ butter (4 tsp)
- 200g _ small tomatoes
- 100g _ lamb's lettuce
- 20g _ sprouts or cress

Instructions. For the pesto, wash the basil, shake dry and cut it into small pieces. Peel and chop the garlic. Using a hand blender, puree the basil, garlic, pine nuts, salt, pepper, and lemon juice with 5 tablespoons of olive oil to a fine pesto. Clean and wash the spinach and puree very finely with the cream. Whisk the eggs, season with salt and pepper, and mix into the spinach cream. Clean and wash the spinach and puree very finely with the cream. Whisk the eggs, season with salt and pepper, and mix into the spinach cream. Melt 1 teaspoon of butter in a non-stick pan. Add 1/4 of the egg mixture and set aside over medium heat for 3-4 minutes. Turn the omelet over and cook for another 3-4 minutes on the other side. Remove and keep warm in a preheated oven at 80 °C (60 °C fan oven; gas: level 1). Make 3 more omelets in this way. Meanwhile, wash, halve and slice the tomatoes for the filling. Clean lamb's lettuce, wash and shake dry. Wash sprouts thoroughly and drain. Cover omelets with lettuce and tomatoes, drizzle with pesto, and sprinkle with sprouts.

3.24 Coconut curry with salmon and sweet potatoes

Preparation: 45 min **Calories:** 549 kcal **Servings:** 4

Ingredients

- 150g _ basmati brown rice
- salt
- 1 onion
- 3 garlic cloves
- 1 red chili pepper
- 20g _ ginger (1 piece)
- 600g _ sweet potatoes (2 sweet potatoes)
- 200g _ celery (3 sticks)
- 20g _ coriander (1 bunch)
- 400g _ salmon fillet
- 1 tsp sesame oil
- 1 tsp cumin
- 1 tsp coriander
- ½ tsp turmeric powder
- 150ml _ coconut milk (9% fat)
- 300ml _ vegetable broth
- 2 tbsp fish sauce

Instructions. Cook the rice 2.5 times the amount of boiling salted water according to package directions for about 35 minutes. Meanwhile, peel the onion and garlic and cut them into small cubes. Halve the chili lengthwise, deseed, wash and chop. Ginger peel and finely chop. Peel sweet potatoes and cut them into cubes. Clean the celeriac, de-thread if necessary, wash and cut into small pieces. Wash the cilantro, shake it dry and pluck off the leaves. Rinse the salmon fillet, pat dry and roughly chop. Heat oil in a pot. Sauté onion, garlic, ginger, and chili for 2-3 minutes over medium heat. Add spices and sauté. Deglaze with coconut milk and broth and bring to a boil. Add the celery and diced sweet potatoes and cook over low heat for 10 minutes. Add salmon and cook another 4-5 minutes. Season coconut curry with fish sauce and serve with rice and coriander.

3.25 Baked potatoes with broccoli

Preparation: 1 hour **Calories:** 471 kcal **Servings:** 4

Ingredients

- 500g _ small new potato
- 3 branches rosemary
- 4 tbsp olive oil
- salt
- pepper
- 1 box garden cress
- 1 tsp lemon juice
- 100g _ cashew butter
- nutmeg
- 600g _ broccoli (1 broccoli)
- 50g _ cashew nuts
- ½ bunch radish
- 1 bunch of spring onions

Instructions. Thoroughly scrub, wash and halve the potatoes. Wash the rosemary, shake it dry and pluck off the needles. Mix everything with 2 tablespoons of olive oil, salt, and pepper. Place the potatoes on a baking tray lined with baking paper and bake in a preheated oven at 200°C (convection oven: 180°C; gas: mark 3) for about 30 minutes. In the meantime, cut the cress from the bed and puree with lemon juice and cashew butter using a hand blender; Gradually add water until the sauce has a creamy consistency. Season with salt, pepper, and freshly grated nutmeg. Clean and wash the broccoli, cut it into bite-sized florets and mix it with the remaining olive oil, salt, and pepper. Add the broccoli florets to the potatoes and bake for another 15 minutes. Meanwhile, toast the cashews in a pan over medium-high heat for 3 minutes until lightly browned. Take out and set aside. Clean and wash the radishes and cut them into fine sticks. Clean, wash and cut the spring onions into rings. Remove the potatoes and broccoli from the oven and arrange on plates. Spread the cashew sauce on top and serve with the cashew nuts, radishes and spring onions.

3.26 Rice bowl with chickpeas and cashew sauce

Preparation: 25 min **Calories:** 615 kcal **Servings:** 2

Ingredients

- 60g _ cashew nuts
- 100g _ long grain rice (parboiled)
- 2 carrots
- 1 bunch radishes (small bunch)
- 100g _ rocket or lamb's lettuce
- 1 orange or apple
- 1 tbsp lime juice
- 10g _ parsley (0.5 bunch)
- Salt
- pepper

- 265g _chickpeas (jar, drained weight)

Instructions. Soak cashew nuts in 100 ml water. Cook rice in boiling salted water according to packet instructions. Meanwhile, peel and grate the carrots. Clean, wash and slice the radishes. Clean and wash the rocket and shake it dry. Peel and chop the orange. Wash the parsley, shake it dry and cut it into small pieces. Puree the cashew nuts with the soaking water, lime juice, and parsley, and season with salt and pepper. Arrange the rice, lettuce, carrots, radishes, chickpeas, and fruit in bowls and serve drizzled with the sauce.

3.27 Avocado and baked egg

Servings: 1
Ingredients
- 1 ripe avocado
- 2 fresh eggs
- Salt
- Pepper
- coriander, chopped chillies or chives to decorate (optional)

Instructions. Preheat the oven to 225°. Cut the avocado in half and remove the seed. With a spoon, remove a little of the meat to make the seed hole bigger and deeper. Place the avocados in a baking dish in which they are in a firm position without moving. Crack one of the eggs into a cup and carefully add the yolk first, then a little of the white. You can do it at once but it might not fit all the egg inside the hole. When you have added both eggs, add salt and pepper and place the tray in the oven. Bake 15 to 20 minutes or until white is set and yolk is soft and creamy. Garnish with coriander leaves, chilli slices or chives.

3.28 Salmon Spinach Pasta

Preparation: 20 min **Calories:** 612 kcal **Servings:** 4
Ingredients
- 500g _ wholemeal pasta (e.g. penne)
- salt
- 1 clove of garlic
- 1 red onion
- 1 organic lemon
- 2 tbsp olive oil
- 300ml _ vegetable broth
- 3 tbsp cream cheese
- 250g _ salmon fillet
- 80g _ spinach
- pepper

Kitchen appliances. 1 pot, 1 knife, 1 work board, 1 grater, 1 pan, 1 salad spinner
Instructions. Cook the noodles in plenty of boiling salted water according to the package instructions. Then drain. In the meantime, peel and finely dice the garlic and onion. Rinse the lemon in hot water, pat dry, and grate the zest.

Heat oil in a pan, sauté garlic and onions over medium heat until translucent. Add lemon zest and pour in vegetable broth. Stir in the cream cheese and bring it to a boil. Then reduce the heat. Cut the salmon fillet into bite-sized pieces, add to the sauce and let it simmer for about 5 minutes. Wash and spin dry the spinach. Add to the salmon with the noodles, season with pepper, and mix well. Divide the salmon pasta with spinach among four plates and serve.

3.29 Herb omelette with smoked salmon

Preparation: 15 minutes **Calories:** 272 kcal **Servings:** 4

Ingredients

- 1 cucumber
- salt
- 100g _ smoked salmon
- 2 boxes cress
- 20g _ dill (1 bunch)
- 6 eggs
- pepper
- 4 tbsp mineral water
- 80g _ kefir (4 tbsp)
- 4 tbsp olive oil

Instructions. Wash the cucumber and cut diagonally into thin slices. Set aside a few cucumber slices, lay the rest flat on plates, and sprinkle with salt. Dice the salmon. Cut the cress from the beds. Wash the dill, shake dry and chop. Whisk eggs with salt, pepper, mineral water, and kefir and stir in dill. Heat 2 tbsp oil in a pan. Add half the egg mixture and cook over low heat for 3-4 minutes to form an omelet. Fry a second omelet with the remaining egg mixture. Top the omelets with diced salmon, cucumber slices, and cress, fold them up, cut them in half, and arrange on the cucumber slices.

3.30 Baked fennel with caramelized grapes

Preparation: 20 min **Ready in:** 50 minutes **Calories:** 314 kcal **Servings:** 4

Ingredients

- 4 tubers fennel
- salt
- pepper
- 2 tbsp olive oil
- 1 clove of garlic
- 4 branches
- thyme
- 30g _ butter
- 40g _ wholemeal breadcrumbs (4 tbsp)
- 30g _ pine nuts (2 tbsp)
- 30g _ roquefort (45% fat in dry matter)
- 200g _ red grapes
- 1 tbsp red wine vinegar

- 2 tbsp honey

Kitchen appliances. 1 knife, 1 baking sheet

Instructions. Wash the fennel thoroughly, cut it in half, remove the core and cut it into quarters. Place the fennel on a baking sheet lined with parchment paper and season with salt and pepper. Drizzle over olive oil. Peel garlic and chop finely. Wash the thyme, shake it dry and pluck off the leaves. Mix the garlic and thyme with the butter, whole wheat breadcrumbs, and pine nuts and pour over the fennel. Tear Roquefort into pieces and also pour over the fennel. Wash the grapes, drain and separate them from the stalks. Halve the grapes and mix them with vinegar and honey. Put the grapes over the fennel and bake in a preheated oven at 200 °C (180 °C fan oven; gas: level 3) for about 30 minutes. Place the gratinated fennel on four plates with the caramelized grapes and serve.

3.31 Salad with eggs and cabbage pesto

Preparation: 35 min **Calories:** 567 kcal **Servings:** 4

Ingredients

- 50g _ almond kernels
- 3 garlic cloves
- 100g _ kale
- 120ml _ olive oil
- salt
- pepper
- 1 avocado
- 2 handfuls salad mix (sorrel, spinach, beetroot leaves)
- 150g _ cauliflower
- 2 carrots
- 40g _ sprouts
- 30g _ sunflower seeds (2 tbsp)
- 4 tbsp apple cider vinegar
- 2 tsp honey
- 50ml _ wine vinegar
- 4 Eggs

Instructions. Toast the almonds in a hot pan over medium-high heat for 3 minutes. Peel and finely chop the garlic. Clean and wash the kale, shake dry, pluck the greens from the leaf veins and chop roughly. Puree everything with 100 ml olive oil with a hand blender to a pesto. Season with salt and pepper. Halve the avocado, remove the stone, scoop out the flesh and cut it into slices. Wash and dry the lettuce mix. Clean and wash Brussels sprouts, separate them into individual leaves, and place them in a large bowl with the salad. Clean, peel and cut the carrots into strips; wash the sprouts. Mix both with cabbage, avocado, lettuce, and sunflower seeds.

Mix the apple cider vinegar, remaining oil, honey, salt, and pepper into a dressing, pour over the ingredients, and mix. Boil 1 liter of water in a saucepan. Pour in the wine vinegar and create a strudel with a wooden spoon. Crack the eggs one at a time into a ladle and slide them into the water. Let the eggs simmer for 4 minutes on low heat. Arrange the salad on plates, place 1 poached egg on each, and top with some pesto.

3.32 Cream of asparagus

Ingredients

- 400 g of fresh asparagus
- 1 small potato
- ½ small sweet onion
- ½ leek
- 600 ml of vegetable broth
- Olive oil
- Salt and pepper

Instructions. Wash the asparagus and cut, with your fingers, the lower end. You have to feel the stem and start where it creaks. Remove the tips and reserve them for the decoration of the plate. Chop the rest of the asparagus. Peel the onion and clean the leek. Chop them fine. Pour a splash of oil into a pot and fry the onion and leek until translucent, about five minutes. Peel the potato and chop it into pieces. Put the potato and asparagus in the pot. Add the broth and cook everything together, over medium-high heat, for about fifteen minutes, until tender. Shred the vegetables. If the cream is somewhat thick, you can add a little more broth and, on the contrary, if it is too liquid, return it to the pot and cook until it thickens. Put a little oil in a frying pan and grill the asparagus tips. Use them to decorate the cream.

3.33 Crispy salmon in almond sauce

Cooking time: 40 minutes **Services:** 2

Ingredients

- 400g fresh salmon
- 150g raw almonds
- 1 egg
- Unrefined sea salt
- Freshly ground black pepper
- For the almond sauce
- 1/4 cup organic almond butter
- 25g butter _
- 170ml milk _
- 25 g ground almond flour
- 1 pinch nutmeg
- Ground black pepper
- Salt to taste
- 4 ml soy sauce or Tamari sauce (Tamari sauce is gluten-free)
- 1ml rice vinegar
- 1 tbsp extra virgin olive oil

Instructions. To make your crispy salmon, start by preheating the oven to 180ºC; Season the salmon fillets with salt and pepper. With a blender, chop the raw almonds, and leave some slightly larger pieces. Add a pinch of salt and pepper to the almonds, and place on a tray to coat the salmon.

For the batter, first, pass the fillets through the beaten egg and then through the almonds. Put the salmon fillets on a baking tray, and bake for 20 minutes or until the almonds are toasted. For the sauce of this crispy salmon, put the butter and extra virgin olive oil in a saucepan and let them melt over low heat. Stir in milk, ground almonds, freshly grated nutmeg, freshly ground black pepper, salt, almond butter, soy sauce, and rice vinegar. Bring to a boil stirring from time to time with the rod, and when it boils, stop stirring, lower the heat and let it thicken. Add to taste on the salmon.

3.34 Cucumber salad
Ingredients
- 1 tomato
- 2 medium cucumbers
- 1 medium carrot
- 1 small green bell pepper
- ½ cup of lamb's lettuce
- ½ cup chopped fresh cilantro
- 2 tablespoons lemon juice
- ¼ cup cashews
- extra virgin olive oil
- Salt and pepper

Instructions. Peel cucumbers and cut them into slices. Put them in a salad bowl. Wash the tomato and cut it into not very large pieces. Remove the skin from the carrot, and take out thin strips with a peeler. Clean and wash the pepper and cut it julienne. Add the tomato, the carrot strips, the pepper, and the canons to the salad bowl. Mix well and season to taste. Combine the chopped cilantro, oil, and lime juice to make the dressing. Pour over salad and stir. Decorate with cashews.

3.35 Anti-inflammatory salad
Ingredients
- 4 cups baby spinach
- 2 ½ cups strawberries
- 1 sliced avocado
- ½ cup chopped basil
- ½ cup toasted pistachios
- ¼ cup olive oil
- 2 tablespoons balsamic vinegar
- 1 clove garlic

Instructions. Wash the spinach and pat dry with kitchen paper. Remove the stems and put them in a bowl. If you prefer, chop the leaves. Add washed and sliced strawberries, sliced avocado, chopped basil, and pistachios. Top with a strawberry dressing. To do it, put half a cup of strawberries, the oil, the vinegar, and a whole peeled clove of garlic through the blender. Beat until creamy, about a minute.

3.36 Roasted cauliflower with spices, almonds and yogurt sauce

Processing time: 45 minutes **Serving:** 2-4

Ingredients

- 1 large cauliflower, 80-100 g
- Raw sliced almonds
- 1 teaspoon fennel seeds
- 1 teaspoon cumin seeds (cumin grains)
- 1 teaspoon coriander seeds (coriander grains)
- 1/2 teaspoon mustard
- Black or yellow peppercorns
- 1/2 teaspoon of black peppercorns
- 2 cloves
- 1 tablespoon of ground turmeric
- 1 pinch of cayenne or hot paprika
- Fresh parsley or coriander
- 1 thick natural yogurt
- 1/2 teaspoon of granulated garlic
- 1/2 lemon
- salt and extra virgin olive oil.

Instructions. Preheat the oven to 160°C and prepare a tray or fountain. Extend the almonds and separate the spices into grains or seeds. Cut the cauliflower into florets and wash very well, draining the water. Toast the almonds and spices for about 5 minutes, observing that they do not burn. Remove and raise the temperature to 220°C. Crush the toasted spices in a mortar or grind with a grinder or chopper. Add the ground turmeric and the cayenne or hot paprika until you have a more or less homogeneous mixture. Place the cauliflower on a large plate or bowl and toss a drizzle of olive oil and a pinch of salt with the spices. Spread on a baking sheet and roast, occasionally stirring, for about 20-25 minutes. It should be al dente, tender on the inside but slightly hard, toasted on the outside. Adjust baking time to personal taste. Drain the yogurt liquid, season with salt and pepper, and add lemon zest, juice, and a little olive oil. Beat well until you have a creamy texture. Wash and chop the parsley or cilantro and serve with the cauliflower, adding the reserved almonds.

3.37 Tuna in mango curry sauce

Processing time: 30 minutes **Servings:** 2 people

Ingredients

- 1/2 sweet onion or 1 spring onion
- 1/2 clove of garlic
- 1 teaspoon curry spice mix
- 1 pinch of cayenne pepper
- 1/2 teaspoon ground turmeric
- 2 tuna fillets
- white wine
- 1 lemon

- 1 medium, ripe and aromatic mango (approximately 200 ml of pulp)
- 1 tablespoon grated coconut
- black pepper
- salt
- parsley or coriander and extra virgin olive oil.

Instructions. I preferred to prepare the mango separately to limit cooking as much as possible for this dish since it was very ripe and did not need to soften any further. Cut in half and extract the pulp with a large spoon, removing the bone. You have to try to take advantage of all the juices. Chop and blend in a food processor or blender with a pinch of salt and the juice of half a lemon. Reserve. Dry the tuna loins with kitchen paper and cut them into blocks of more or less the same size. Chop the onion and the garlic clove. Heat a little olive oil in a frying pan or saucepan and add both ingredients and spices. Brown until the onion is transparent over low heat, and add a pinch of salt. Add the tuna, season with salt and pepper, and drizzle with the wine. Cook for a few minutes over high heat until the fish is browned on both sides. Add the mango to the pan, lower the heat and stir well. Add the rest of the lemon juice to the grated coconut. Taste the sauce and season more if necessary. Cook until it reduces as desired, adding a little more wine or water if it gets too dry. Serve with finely chopped parsley or cilantro.

3.38 Red sage, grapes and pine nuts Salad with grilled goat cheese
Total time: 20m **Servings:** 2
Ingredients
- Assorted sprouts with red sage 150g _
- Pinions 20g _
- Goat roll cheese in two slices 20g _
- Red grapes 12
- Apple vinegar
- extra virgin olive oil

Instructions. Wash and drain the sprouts and sage well, so the salad does not turn soggy. Wash, dry, and cut the grapes into slices. We distribute in a serving tray or individual bowls the varied shoots and the red sage as a base, and on top, we distribute the grapes and the pine nuts. Separately, heat a griddle over high heat and cut the goat roll into slices of about 4 cm, more or less, on each side. We can also use a kitchen torch, which will take less time. We distribute the goat cheese on the salad and dress to our liking. As this salad is a bit sweet, I recommend a rather acidic dressing to contrast the flavors.

3.39 Eggplant, tomato and spinach curry
Cooking: 25 min **Servings:** 4
Ingredients
- Onion 1
- Garlic clove 2
- Fresh ginger 50 g
- Cayenne Pepper 1
- Ground cumin 10 g

- Garam masala 10 g
- Ground coriander 10 g
- Ground turmeric 5 g
- Concentrated tomato 75 g
- Sunflower oil 50 g
- Eggplant 2
- Tomato 2
- Fresh spinach 80 g
- Vegetables soup 300 ml
- Extra virgin olive oil
- Salt

Instructions. In a food processor, grind the onion, peeled and chopped, the garlic cloves, peeled, the fresh ginger, also peeled, the cayenne pepper, without the seeds (which is what itches), the cumin, the garam masala, coriander, turmeric, concentrated tomato, and sunflower oil. We stop and reserve when we have a homogeneous paste without remains or bumps of any ingredient. Wash the eggplant and tomatoes. Cut the first into approximately 2 cm cubes and the tomatoes into eight segments. Wash the spinach and reserve. Heat a couple of tablespoons of olive oil in a large saucepan and add the reserved pasta. Add the diced aubergine, stir and cook for 10 minutes over low heat. Add the vegetable broth and cook gently for 30 minutes. Add the tomatoes and cook for 10 more minutes. Finally, add the spinach and let it cook for a few minutes until it softens. Season to taste and serve immediately with fresh cilantro sprinkled on top.

3.40 Matcha latte or green tea with milk

Servings: 1

Ingredients
- 1 1/2 tsp matcha green tea powder
- 2-3 tablespoons of hot water
- 1 teaspoon of sugar (optional)
- 1 cup of milk (animal or vegetable)

Instructions. Sprinkle the matcha tea in a cup or bowl. Next, add a little hot water, but not boiling, so it does not burn the tea, and gently whisk until it dissolves. The Japanese use a whisk called 'chasen,' made of bamboo, but we can use any other tool.

Heat the milk without letting it boil and pour little by little over the cup with the matcha dissolved in water. If you want it to be foamy, with the help of an electric mixer, foam the milk and then pour the foam over the cup. Note: vegetable drinks, such as oatmeal or almond, do not create foam, so the drink will be less creamy but just as rich.

3.41 Roasted Salmon with SpiInstant pot lentil soup

Preparation time: 25 minutes **Cooking time**: 15 minutes **Servings**: 8

Device: Instant Pot 6 qt

Ingredients
- one pound of ground beef

- two cloves of minced garlic
- one diced onion
- one spoon of olive oil
- one cup chopped celery
- one cup carrots, chopped
- one large baking potato, peeled and diced
- one cup of lentils
- 6 glasses of beef broth
- 28 oz diced tomatoes with juices
- one spoon of Worcestershire sauce
- one teaspoon of Italian seasoning
- salt and pepper to taste
- fresh parsley and parmesan for decoration optional

Instructions. Turn 6QT Instant Pot over to sauté. Cook beef, onion and garlic until browned and no longer pink. If there is more than 1 tablespoon, drain off the fat. While the beef is browning, prepare the vegetables. Add the beef stock and scrape up any brown bits on the bottom of the pan. Add remaining ingredients. Set the Instant Pot on high pressure for 15 minutes. Once the Instant Pot has been boiling for 15 minutes, let it cool down naturally for 10 minutes. Release remaining pressure. Serve with parmesan and parsley to taste.

3.42 Quinoa salad with avocado and kale
Preparation: 25 min **Cooking:** 15 min **Ready in:** 40 min **Servings:** 4
Ingredients:
- 110g of quinoa
- 300ml of water
- 1 bunch of black cabbage leaves cut into strips
- 1/2 avocado, sliced
- 70g of diced cucumbers
- 50g diced red pepper
- 2 tablespoons of sliced red onion
- 1 tablespoon of crumbled feta

Instructions. Collect the water and quinoa in a saucepan and bring them to a boil. Lower the heat to low, cover, and cook until the quinoa is tender and has absorbed all the water, about 15-20 minutes. Shell and set aside to cool. Place the black cabbage in a pan with 3cm of boiling water in a steaming basket. Cover and steam until hot, about 45 seconds. Transfer to a bowl and add quinoa, avocado, cucumbers, red pepper, red onion, and feta. Mix oil, lemon juice, mustard, salt, and pepper. Pour them over the salad, mix and serve.

3.43 Roasted Sweet Potatoes with Avocado Dip
Preparation time: 25 Minutes **Cooking time:** 40 Minutes **Serving:** 4 Persons

Ingredients
- 1 avocado (halved and pitted)

- 2 large sweet potatoes (washed and cubed)
- 1 lime (juice)
- 4 tablespoons water
- 1 large clove of garlic (peeled and chopped)
- 1/2 teaspoon sea salt (divided)
- 1 teaspoon olive oil
- 2 tablespoons olive oil

Instructions. Turn the oven temperature up to 400 degrees F. Use parchment paper to line a baking sheet. Place the diced potatoes in an equal layer on the prepared baking sheet. Use 2 tbsp of olive oil to drizzle. To ensure that all of the potato pieces get a coating of oil, you should turn them over. Use a third of the salt for seasoning. Put it in the oven for 40-45 minutes, or until it's a golden brown. Put the avocados, garlic, lime juice, and the remaining ½ of the salt in a blender and mix until smooth. Combine until the point of smoothness. Stir in the olive oil and the water gradually. Make sure everything is well combined by continuing to blend. Prepare a dip to accompany the cooked potatoes and serve.

Nutrition Calories: 188 Kcal, Proteins: 3g, Fat: 13g, Carbohydrates: 20g

3.44 Chicken with Lemon and Asparagus
Preparation time: 15 Minutes **Cooking time:** 20 Minutes **Serving:** 4 Persons

Ingredients

- 2 cups asparagus (chopped)
- 1 pound of chicken breasts (boneless and skinless)
- 1/4 cup flour
- 2 lemons (sliced)
- 4 tablespoons butter (divided)
- 1 teaspoon lemon pepper seasoning
- 1/2 teaspoon salt
- 1/2 teaspoon pepper

Instructions. Lemons and Asparagus: The remaining butter should be melted in the same pan over moderate heat. Pour in the asparagus. Heat until the vegetables are crisp-tender. Remove from the stove. Place the lemon slices in a single layer on the hot skillet. Caramelization is achieved by cooking for a few minutes on each side without stirring. Remove from the stovetop. **Chicken:** To make slices that are just 3/4 of an inch thick, cut each chicken chest in half lengthwise. Put the flour, salt, and pepper into a wide, shallow dish. Combine in a harmonious manner. Sprinkle the flour mixture over each piece of chicken. Prepare the first ½ of the butter by melting it in a pan over medium heat. Place the chicken pieces within. To get a golden brown color, cook for Five minutes for each side. While cooking, season both sides of the chicken using lime pepper. Putting aside. **Assembly:** Arrange the cooked asparagus, lemon, and chicken in tiers on a serving plate. Serve.

Nutrition Calories: 250 Kcal, Proteins: 13g, Fat: 7g, Carbohydrates: 26g

3.45 Shrimp Fajitas

Preparation time: 25 Minutes **Cooking time:** 25 Minutes **Serving:** 4 Persons

Ingredients

- 1 red bell pepper (sliced thinly)
- 1 1/2 pounds of shrimp
- 1 yellow bell pepper
- 1 small red onion
- 1 orange bell pepper
- 1 1/2 tablespoons extra virgin olive oil
- 1 teaspoon kosher salt
- 2 teaspoons chili powder
- 1/2 teaspoon onion powder
- Fresh cilantro (for garnish)
- 1/2 teaspoon smoked paprika
- 1/2 teaspoon garlic powder
- 1/2 teaspoon ground cumin
- Lime
- Freshly ground pepper
- Tortillas (warmed)

Instructions. The oven should be preheated at 450 degrees F. Spray cooking spray onto a baking sheet. Put the shrimp, peppers, onions, spices, olive oil, and salt into a large mixing bowl. Make sure to give it a good toss. Distribute them in a single layer on the baking sheet. Put in oven and bake for 10 min. Go ahead and turn the oven to broil. To finish cooking the fajita, wait 2 minutes. Lime juice should be squeezed over the fajita. Use cilantro as a garnish. Put on heated tortillas and serve.

Nutrition Calories: 241 Kcal, Proteins: 14g, Fat: 10g, Carbohydrates: 25g

3.46 Mediterranean One Pan Cod

Preparation time: 15 Minutes **Cooking time:** 20 Minutes **Serving:** 4 Persons

Ingredients

- 2 cups fennel (sliced)
- 2 cups kale (shredded)
- 1 cup fresh tomatoes (diced)
- 1/2 cup water

- 1 cup oil-cured black olives
- 1 pound cod (quartered)
- 1 can (14.5 ounces) diced tomato
- 1 small onion (sliced)
- 3 large cloves of garlic (chopped)
- Pinch of red pepper (crushed)
- 1 teaspoon orange zest
- 2 tablespoons olive oil
- 1/2 teaspoon dried oregano
- 1/4 teaspoon black pepper
- 1/4 teaspoon fennel seeds
- 1/8 teaspoon salt

Garnish:

- Orange zest
- Fresh oregano
- Fennel fronds
- Olive oil

Instructions. The olive oil should be heated in a pan over medium heat. Fennel, onion, and garlic should be cooked together for 8 minutes. You may add salt and pepper to taste. Incorporate the tinned tomatoes, water, fresh tomatoes, and kale. Just add 12 additional minutes of cooking time. Add the oregano, pepper, and olives, and stir to combine. Toss the fish with a mixture of pepper, fennel seeds, salt, and lemon or lime juice. Place the fish fillets in the tomato sauce. Tightly cover the skillet. Ten minutes at a low simmer. Garnish. Serve.

Nutrition Calories: 333 Kcal, Proteins: 43g, Fat: 10g, Carbohydrates: 19g

3.47 Garlic Tomato Basil Chicken

Preparation time: 20 Minutes **Cooking time:** 15 Minutes **Serving:** 4 Persons

Ingredients

- 4 medium zucchini (spiralized)
- 1 pound of chicken breasts (boneless and skinless)
- Salt
- 1 cup fresh basil (loosely packed and cut into ribbons)
- 3 garlic cloves (minced)
- Pepper
- 14.5-ounce can of chopped tomatoes
- 1/2 yellow onion (diced)

- 1/4 teaspoon red pepper flakes (crushed)
- 2 tablespoons olive oil (divided)

Instructions. Use plastic wrap to enclose each chicken breast. Beat them to a uniform thickness of one inch. Tear open each chicken breast. You may add salt and pepper to taste. Place a teaspoon of olive oil in a pan and heat it over medium heat. Chicken breasts should be placed. Brown them in a pan and cook them all the way through. Putting aside. Put the leftover olive oil in the same pan and heat it over medium. Keep the onion cooking for around 5 minutes, and add the garlic. Keep sautéing for another minute. Add the tomatoes and basil and mix well. Add some crushed red pepper, black pepper, and salt to taste. Put it on low heat and mix it every so often for 10 minutes. Mix in the chicken breasts and zoodles. Allow to heat slowly for a couple of moments. Serve.

Nutrition Calories: 686 Kcal, Proteins: 34g, Fat: 40g, Carbohydrates: 46g

3.48 Asian Garlic Noodles

Preparation time: 05 Minutes **Cooking time:** 10 Minutes **Serving:** 4 Persons

Ingredients

Noodles:

- 1 small red bell pepper (minced)
- 1 large spaghetti squash
- 1/2 cup fresh cilantro (diced)
- 1/2 large carrot (julienne cut)
- 1/4 cup roasted cashews (chopped)
- 1/2 medium zucchini (julienne cut)

Sauce:

- 6 garlic cloves
- 6 large Medjool dates (pitted)
- 2 tablespoons fish sauce
- 1/4 cup coconut milk (full fat)
- 2 tablespoons red curry paste
- 2/3 cup coconut aminos
- 2 tablespoons fresh ginger (grated)

Instructions. Please preheat your microwave to 425 degrees F. Make a horizontal cut across the spaghetti squash. Remove the pulp by scraping it. Arrange the spaghetti squash cut-side up on a baking sheet. Olive oil should be brushed over the exposed area. Set the oven timer for 30 min. A noodle-like texture may be achieved by scraping the flesh with a fork. To make the sauce, throw all the ingredients into a blender. Puree. Throw all the noodle-making stuff into a bowl and mix it together. Cover the noodles with the sauce. Combine in a harmonious manner.

Nutrition Calories: 426 Kcal, Proteins: 30g, Fat: 7g, Carbohydrates: 62g

3.49 Roasted cauliflower soup with curry and lemon
Preparation: 10 minutes **Cooking:** 30 minutes **Servings:** 3/4
Ingredients

- 1 Cauliflower (about 600g)
- 250 ml Fresh liquid cream
- 2 tsp Vegetable broth (granular)
- 1/2 Lemon (Juice)
- 1 tablespoon Curry
- 1 tsp Garlic powder
- 2 tablespoons Extra virgin olive oil
- Salt

Instructions. Start preparing the roasted cauliflower cream by removing the outer leaves from the cauliflower and dividing it into fairly small rosettes. Arrange them on a baking sheet covered with parchment paper and season with salt, garlic powder, curry, lemon juice, and EVO oil. Bake in a ventilated oven at 200 ° C for 20 minutes. After this time, put the roasted cauliflower rosettes in a pan with the cream and blend everything with an immersion blender. If the mixture is too thick, add a little water. Also, add the granular vegetable broth and cook for about 10 minutes over medium heat. Serve the soup of roasted cauliflower immediately by adding the chili powder and raw EVO oil to taste.

3.50 Leek and cheese omelette
Ingredients:

- 1 small leek
- 1 spring onion
- 250 ml of light cooking cream
- a piece of raw goat cheese
- 3-4 fresh organic eggs
- pink salt
- extra virgin coconut oil

Instructions. Grease the bottom of a non-stick pan and offer the leek and spring onion, cut into thin slices, for 10 minutes. Meanwhile, in a deep dish, beat the eggs, both egg white and yolk, with a little salt, then add the cream and mix well again, until the mixture is smooth. Insert the cheese cut into small cubes and pour it all over the leek and spring onion in the pan. Cook over low heat for about 6-7 minutes. Subsequently, using a lid of adequate diameter to cover the entire pan, turn the omelette and continue to cook for another 6-7 minutes.

3.51 Asia pointed cabbage edamame pan

Working time: 10 min **Completed in:** 20 min **Calories:** 482 **Servings:** 3

Ingredients

- Cabbage 1 piece / 1000g
- Edamame (frozen) 200 grams
- Vine tomato/s 3 pieces / 600g
- Onion 1pc /100g
- Tomato paste 3 tablespoons / 30g
- Olive oil 3 tablespoons / 25g
- Vegan Sausages 180 grams
- Turmeric 2 teaspoons / 4g
- Black cumin (whole grains) 2 teaspoons / 6g
- Salt
- Pepper

Instructions. Remove the outer leaves of the pointed cabbage. Quarter the cabbage, cut it into strips, and wash. Peel and chop the onion. Wash and dice the tomato. Cut vegan sausages into bite-sized pieces. Heat olive oil in a large pan, add onion, and sauté for 2 minutes. Add the pointed cabbage, reduce the heat slightly and fry for about 5 minutes. Stir occasionally. Add edamame and cook for another 5 minutes until the cabbage is done. Add the tomato pieces, turmeric, vegan sausages, and tomato paste, mix well, season with salt and pepper and continue to simmer for 2-3 minutes. Arrange on plates and sprinkle with black cumin.

3.52 Fried sauerkraut with parsley quark

Preparation: 45 min **Calories:** 317 kcal **Servings:** 4

Ingredients

- 400g _ sweet potatoes (1 sweet potato)
- 100g _ red onions (2 red onions)

- 500g _ fresh sauerkraut
- 40g _ almond sticks
- 1 tbsp rapeseed oil
- 100ml _ classic vegetable broth
- 70g _ raisins
- 1 bunch flat leaf parsley
- 300g _ low-fat quark
- Iodized salt with fluoride
- Cayenne pepper

Kitchen appliances. 1 work board, 1 peeler, 1 vegetable slicer, 1 small knife, 1 sieve, 1 small pan, 1 large pan, 1 wooden spoon, 1 measuring cup, 1 small bowl, 1 tablespoon, 1 spatula.

Instructions. Peel the sweet potato with a vegetable peeler, rinse and use a mandolin to slice into long, very fine strips. Peel onions, halve and cut into strips. Drain the sauerkraut in a colander. Roast the almond sticks in a pan without fat until golden brown and leave to cool. Heat oil in a large skillet or wok. Add the onion strips and sauté briefly. Add the sweet potato and fry on low heat for 5 minutes, turning frequently. Gradually pour in the vegetable broth. Add the sauerkraut and raisins to the vegetables. Fry over low heat for 15 minutes, turning occasionally. Meanwhile, wash the parsley, shake dry and pluck off the leaves; set aside some and chop the rest very finely. Mix the low-fat quark with the chopped parsley, salt, and cayenne pepper in a small bowl. Season the sauerkraut with salt and cayenne pepper. Sprinkle with slivers of almonds, garnish with the remaining parsley and serve with the parsley quark.

3.53 Diced chicken with leek and lemon

Ingredients
- 400 g straight of diced chicken
- leek cut into slices
- 1 organic lemon
- pink salt
- extra virgin coconut oil

Instructions. Fry the sliced leek in coconut oil and then add the diced chicken. Sauté for 5 minutes, and then add the juice of half a lemon and a few pieces of grated peel. If necessary, add water to finish cooking.

3.54 Almond crusted avocado and bulgur tomato salad

Preparation: 20 min **Calories:** 559 kcal **Servings:** 2

Ingredients
- 120g _ bulgur
- Salt
- 60g _ rocket (0.75 bunch)
- 100g _ cherry tomatoes
- 200g _ avocado (1 avocado)
- Pepper
- 20g _ chopped almonds (1 heaped tbsp)

- 3 tbsp white wine vinegar
- 6 tbsp classic vegetable broth
- 1 tsp honey
- 1 tbsp olive oil

Kitchen appliances. 1 tablespoon, 1 teaspoon, 1 small knife, 1 large knife, 1 work board, 1 small bowl, 1 large bowl, 1 salad servers, 1 salad spinner, 1 grill pan, 1 plate, 1 spatula, 1 fork, 1 saucepan.

Instructions. Cook bulgur according to package instructions in boiling salted water. Meanwhile, trim and wash the rocket, spin it dry and roughly chop. Wash and quarter the tomatoes. Halve the avocado, remove the stone, and season the cut surfaces with salt and pepper. Place the almonds on a plate. Press the cut side of the avocado halves into the almonds.

Heat a grill pan. Place the avocado halves cut side down and fry over low heat for 2-3 minutes. Whisk together the vinegar, vegetable stock, honey, and olive oil, and season with salt and pepper. Fluff up the bulgur with a fork and place it in a bowl. Add tomatoes and arugula. Pour the dressing over. Mix everything well and season with salt and pepper. Serve the bulgur tomato salad with the grilled avocado halves.

3.55 Quick lentil turmeric bowl

Working time: 15 minutes **Completed in:** 15 minutes **Calories:** 483 **Servings:** 2

Ingredients

- MyMüsli Lentil Turmeric Porridge 130 grams
- Water 400 grams
- Paprika 1 piece / 150g
- Avocado/s (ready to eat) 1 piece / 250g
- basil (fresh) 2 branch/s / 10 g
- Balsamic vinegar 2 tablespoons / 16g
- olive oil (virgin) 2 tablespoons / 16g
- Spring onions ½ piece / 30 g

Instructions. Put the lentils turmeric porridge with 400ml water in a saucepan, bring to a boil and simmer for 3 minutes. Microwave (without cooking) Mix porridge with water and heat in the microwave for about 1.5 minutes (at 600W). Meanwhile, wash and remove the basil from the stems. Halve, deseed and remove the avocado from the skin. Wash the peppers, deseed and cut into bite-sized cubes or fine strips. Wash the spring onion and cut into fine rings. Divide the finished lentil turmeric porridge between 2 bowls and garnish with the diced peppers, spring onions, avocado & basil. Then drizzle with 1 tablespoon each of olive oil and balsamic vinegar, and your quick takeaway meal is ready!

3.56 Shrimp Garlic Zoodles

Preparation time: 15 Minutes **Cooking time:** 05 Minutes **Serving:** 4 Persons

Ingredients

- 2 medium zucchini
- 3/4 pounds medium shrimp

- 4 cloves garlic (minced)
- Salt
- Red pepper flakes
- 1 tablespoon olive oil
- Zest and juice of 1 lemon
- Fresh parsley (chopped)
- Pepper

Instructions. Cook the zoodles in a spiralizer set to medium. Putting aside. Stir the olive oil, lime zest, and lime juice together in a pan over moderate heat. The shrimp should be added and stirred in. Keep it in the oven for a couple of minutes. Put the crushed red pepper and garlic in a bowl and stir them in. Keep cooking for another minute. Start cooking the zoodles. Three minutes of tossing should be enough time to get a medium-rare consistency. You may add salt and pepper to taste. Dress with chopped parsley. Serve.

Nutrition Calories: 286 Kcal, Proteins: 27g, Fat: 5.7g, Carbohydrates: 8.1g

3.57 Cauliflower Grits and Shrimp

Preparation time: 15 Minutes **Cooking time:** 05 Minutes **Serving:** 4 Persons

Ingredients

Cauliflower Grits:

- 1 large clove of garlic (chopped)
- 1 bag (12 ounces) of frozen cauliflower
- Salt
- 2 tablespoons butter

Shrimp:

- 3 tablespoons Cajun seasoning (no salt)
- 1 pound large shrimp (peeled and deveined)
- 2 tablespoons butter
- Salt

Instructions. The cauliflower and the garlic should be steamed together in a pot. Waiting to be steamed till soft. (The piping hot liquid should not be thrown away.) Put the garlic, steamed cauliflower, and butter in a food processor. The consistency may be adjusted throughout processing. If you want a thinner or thicker consistency, add additional hot water and salt and mix again. Putting aside. Combine the Cajun seasonings in a bowl. Sprinkling the spice on the shrimp is not enough. Put some salt on it. Butter should be melted in a pan over medium heat. Add the shrimp. Cook until the internal temperature of the meat reaches 160 F. Divide the grits into 2 bowls and top with the cauliflower. Place the shrimp on top once they have been cooked. When serving, transfer the gravy from the pan to the bowls. Serve.

Nutrition Calories: 350 Kcal, Proteins: 37g, Fat: 16g, Carbohydrates: 21g

3.58 Green Curry

Preparation time: 20 Minutes **Cooking time:** 15 Minutes **Serving:** 4 Persons

Ingredients

- 12 ounces tofu (firm)
- 3 cups broccoli florets
- A swish of olive oil
- 3 cans (14 ounces) of coconut milk
- 2 sweet potatoes (peeled and cubed)
- 4 tablespoons green curry paste
- A sprinkle of salt

Garnish:

- Fresh cilantro (chopped)
- Fish sauce
- Golden raisins
- Brown sugar

Instructions. Use towels to rinse the tofu. Cube the tofu and set it aside. Put the olive oil in a pan and warm it over moderate heat. Toss the tofu in the pan. Put some salt on it. Cook the tofu in hot oil for fifteen min, occasionally turning until it is golden brown all over. Putting aside. Mix the curry paste, coconut milk, and sweet potatoes in the same saucepan and heat over medium. Hold at a low boil for ten min. Add the broccoli and tofu to the pan. Simmer for another 5 minutes. Flourish. Serve.

Nutrition Calories: 328 Kcal, Proteins: 24g, Fat: 20g, Carbohydrates: 17g

CHAPTER 4: Anti-Inflammatory Dinner Recipes

4.1 Stir-Fried Snap Pea and Chicken

Preparation time: 20 Minutes **Cooking time:** 15 Minutes **Serving:** 4 Persons

Ingredients

- 2 1/2 cups snap peas
- 1 1/4 cups chicken breast (skinless, boneless, and sliced thinly)
- 1 bunch of scallions (sliced thinly)
- 2 tablespoons vegetable oil
- 1 red bell pepper (sliced thinly)
- 3 tablespoons fresh cilantro
- 2 tablespoons sesame seeds (+ more for garnish)
- 3 tablespoons soy sauce
- 2 tablespoons rice vinegar
- Freshly ground black pepper
- 2 garlic cloves (minced)
- Salt
- 2 teaspoons Sriracha

Instructions. Put the oil in a pan and heat it over medium heat. The scallions and garlic should be sautéed for a minute. Cooked snap peas and red bell pepper should be added to the pot. Add some oil and saute for three minutes. Drop the chicken in there. Add another 5 minutes of cooking time. Combine the rice vinegar, sesame seeds, soy sauce, and Sriracha. Put everything in a bowl and mix it together. Wait 2 minutes while it simmers. Incorporate the chopped cilantro. Stir. Sprinkle some sesame seeds and chopped cilantro over each dish. Serve.

Nutrition Calories: 261 Kcal, Proteins: 29g, Fat: 10g, Carbohydrates: 14g

4.2 Turkey Chili with Avocado

Preparation time: 25 Minutes **Cooking time:** 22 Minutes **Serving:** 8 Persons

Ingredients

- 4 cups chicken broth
- 1 pound ground turkey
- 1 can (15 ounces) of white beans
- 1 large white onion (diced)
- 1 can (15 ounces) of corn kernels
- 1 avocado (diced)

- Freshly ground black pepper

- 2 tablespoons extra-virgin olive oil

- 4 garlic cloves (minced)

- 2 teaspoons ground cumin

- 1 teaspoon ground coriander

- 1 teaspoon cayenne pepper

- Salt

Instructions. Put the olive oil in a pan and warm it over moderate flame. Put the onion in a pan and cook it for 8 minutes. Blend in the garlic. Maintain the low heat for one more minute of sauteing. Place the turkey inside. To ensure thorough cooking, set the timer for 7 minutes. Spice it up with cayenne, cumin, coriander, pepper, and salt. Stir. Maintain heat for a few minutes. Add the broth to the pot. The ingredients should be left to cook at a low simmer for 35 minutes. Prepare the maize and beans. Keep at a low boil for a further 3 minutes. Add some chopped avocado to the top of each dish. Serve.

Nutrition Calories: 686 Kcal, Proteins: 47g, Fat: 46g, Carbohydrates: 14g

4.3 Poached salmon with rice and papaya

Preparation: 50 min **Calories:** 451 kcal **Servings:** 4

Ingredients

- 200g _ brown rice
- salt
- 2 organic limes
- 30g _ ginger (1 piece)
- 1 stem lemongrass (only the light part)
- 400g _ salmon fillet (with skin)
- 2 tbsp fish sauce or soy sauce
- 1 tsp sesame oil
- 1 red chili pepper
- 2 spring onions
- 5g _ mint (1 handful)
- 5g _ coriander (1 handful)
- 40g _ sprout mix
- 1 papaya
- 600g _ small cucumber (2 small organic cucumbers)
- pepper

Instructions. Cook the rice twice the amount of boiling salted water for 30-40 minutes. Meanwhile, rinse the limes in hot water, cut 1 fruit into slices, and squeeze the others; set the juice aside. Peel the ginger, slice 1 half and finely chop the other half. Remove the husks from the lemongrass and cut them into small pieces. In a large pan, boil 1 liter of water with the lime, ginger slices, and lemongrass.

Rinse salmon fillet, place skin side down in stock and poach over low heat for 10-12 minutes. Meanwhile, mix the lime juice with the fish sauce, sesame oil, and chopped ginger. Halve the chili pepper lengthways, deseed, wash, cut into fine rings and add to the seasoning sauce. Clean and wash the spring onions and cut them into fine rings. Wash the herbs, shake dry and pluck off the leaves. Scald the sprouts in hot water and drain. Halve the papaya, deseed, peel and slice crosswise. Wash the cucumbers, halve lengthways, and cut diagonally into long strips. Remove the salmon fillet from the poaching broth, remove the skin and roughly chop. Arrange the rice with sprouts, salmon, cucumber, and papaya slices on plates, sprinkle with herbs and drizzle with a little seasoning sauce; Serve the remaining seasoning sauce separately.

4.4 Kale pesto with hazelnuts
Preparation: 20 min **Calories:** 219 kcal **Servings:** 8
Ingredients
- 200g _ kale
- salt
- 2 garlic cloves
- 120g _ hazelnut kernels
- 1 tbsp lemon juice
- pepper
- 100ml _ olive oil

Instructions. Clean and wash the kale, remove the hard stalks and roughly chop. Cook the cabbage in boiling salted water for about 2-3 minutes, rinse in cold water, and shake well to dry. Peel and finely chop the garlic. Puree the kale with hazelnuts, garlic, lemon juice, salt, pepper, and oil to form a creamy pesto. Season with salt and pepper.

4.5 Arugula Salad with Turmeric Cauliflower
Preparation: 30 min **Calories:** 221 kcal **Servings:** 4
Ingredients
- 800g _ small cauliflower (1 small cauliflower)
- 1 tbsp turmeric powder
- salt
- 200g _ red peppers (1 red pepper)
- 200g _ yellow peppers (1 yellow pepper)
- 150g _ pineapple pulp
- 1 lemon
- 1 avocado
- 80g _ rocket (1 bunch)
- 200g _ oranges (1 orange)
- 150g _ yoghurt (1.5% fat)
- pepper
- chili flakes

Instructions. Clean the cauliflower, cut it in half, cut out the stalk, wash the cauliflower, cut it into florets and cook with the turmeric in boiling salted water over medium heat for about 10 minutes. Halve, deseed, wash and dice the peppers. Cut the pineapple into small cubes. Halve the lemon and squeeze the juice. Halve and stone the avocado, lift the flesh out of the skin, cut it into strips and sprinkle with half the lemon juice. Wash the rocket and shake it dry. Peel the orange to remove all white; Cut out the fruit fillets between the membranes, catching the juice. Mix the yogurt with the remaining lemon juice, orange juice, salt, and pepper. Mix the cauliflower, bell pepper, pineapple, avocado, and rocket, divide into bowls, drizzle with dressing and sprinkle with chili flakes.

4.6 Oriental Style Salad

Ingredients

- 2 courgettes
- 1 celery
- 1 bunch of black grapes
- 2 carrots
- 1 spring onion
- ½ lemon juice
- 30 grams of peeled walnuts
- 1 apple
- 2 tablespoons of soy sauce
- 1 tablespoon of oil
- pepper and salt.

Instructions. Clean and cut the celery, courgettes, carrots, and spring onions into thin sticks; see the post on the art of cutting vegetables. Heat the oil in a frying pan or wok and add the spring onion and carrots; sauté the whole for 5 minutes. Add the courgettes to the pan and continue cooking for 3 more minutes, then season with a little salt. Add the lemon juice and the soybeans, stir everything together and cook for 1 more minute. Remove the pan from the heat but keep it warm. Wash and cut the apple into small segments removing the core, and cut the grape grains in half, removing the seeds. Now you have to mix both fruits with the contents of the pan in a salad bowl and sprinkle the whole with the nuts a little chopped.

4.7 Beef and Ginger Skillet

Preparation: 20 min **Calories:** 571 kcal **Servings:** 4

Ingredients

- 500g _ beef sirloin steak
- 40g _ ginger (1 piece)
- 2 garlic cloves
- 4 tbsp teriyaki sauce
- 2 tsp food starch
- 250g _ sugar snap
- 2 red peppers
- 3 tbsp sesame oil

- 250ml _ meatsoup
- 250g _ mie noodles or other Asian noodles
- 1 tbsp lemon juice
- Salt
- Pepper

Instructions. Rinse beef, pat dry, and cut into thin strips. Peel and chop the ginger and garlic. Mix 3 tablespoons of teriyaki sauce, starch, and half of ginger and garlic. Let the meat marinate for 10 minutes. Meanwhile, trim and wash sugar snap peas. Halve the peppers, deseed, wash and cut into strips. Heat oil in a large pan. Sear the meat for 3 minutes over high heat. Remove from the pan and set aside. Add the vegetables to the drippings along with the remaining ginger and garlic and sauté over medium-high heat for 4 minutes. Deglaze with the remaining teriyaki sauce. Add snow peas and broth and cook over medium heat for 4-5 minutes. While the vegetables are cooking, cook the noodles in plenty of boiling salted water until al dente, according to the package instructions. Pour in a colander and let drain. Add the meat to the vegetables, heat for 2 minutes over medium heat, and season with lemon juice, salt, and pepper.

4.8 Mackerel fillets on peppers and capers with bread

Preparation: 35 min **Calories:** 461 kcal **Servings:** 4

Ingredients

- Red peppers
- 2 yellow peppers
- 1 red onion
- 3 tbsp olive oil
- salt
- pepper
- 500g _ mackerel fillet (4 mackerel fillets)
- 200g _ wholemeal bread (4 slices)
- 10g _ parsley (0.5 bunch)
- 60g _ capers (jar; 4 tbsp)

Instructions. Halve the peppers, deseed, wash and cut lengthways into strips approx. 1 cm wide. Peel the onion, halve it, and cut it into thin strips. Mix the pepper and onion strips in a bowl with 2 tbsp olive oil, salt, and pepper. Heat a grill pan. In a grill pan, sauté the vegetables over medium-high heat for about 5-7 minutes. Then season the vegetables with salt and pepper, remove from the pan, and keep warm. While the vegetables are cooking, rinse and pat dry the mackerel fillets and season with salt and pepper. Heat the remaining oil in the grill pan. Fry the mackerel fillets over medium-high heat for about 3-5 minutes per side. Take out of the pan and let it steep. Meanwhile, toast the bread slices in the pan over medium heat without fat for 2 minutes per side. Wash the parsley, shake it dry and pluck off the leaves. Spread the grilled vegetables with capers and parsley on the bread slices and place the mackerel fillets on top.

4.9 Cauliflower based pizza
Ingredients
For the base:
- 450 gr cauliflower (half cauliflower)
- 1 tbsp chia and flax seeds (previously soaked for at least 5 hours)
- 1/2 cup water
- Salt
- garlic powder
- oregano
- Pepper
- grated Parmesan cheese

Toppings:
- homemade tomato sauce
- fresh mushrooms
- canned sardines
- Cherry tomatoes
- mozzarella cheese
- fresh spinach
- fresh basil

Instructions. Mash the cauliflower until it has a couscous-like texture. Put the cauliflower in a pan with 1 glass of water and a little salt and let it simmer for about 15 minutes. Let it cool down. Pour into a clean cloth and press to squeeze out as much water as possible. In a bowl, place the cauliflower and mix with the soaked flax and chia seeds, salt, pepper, garlic powder, cheese, and a little oregano. Mix well. Place the dough between two baking papers on the oven tray and give it a round shape with the help of a rolling pin. Put in the oven preheated to 200°C and let it cook for about 30 minutes in the middle part. Remove and flip to bake on the other side. Place the toppings: homemade tomato sauce, cheese, spinach, sliced mushrooms, cherry tomatoes, and sardines. Bake again until the cheese is melted and the rest of the ingredients are cooked (about 10 minutes). Garnish with a few fresh basil leaves.

4.10 Warm Salad with Pine Nuts, Tomato and Basil
Servings 4:
Ingredients
- 400g mixed baby sprouts
- 8 pear tomatoes
- 1 clove garlic
- 4 sprigs of basil
- 2 tablespoons balsamic vinegar
- 1 purple onion
- 20g peeled pine nuts
- extra virgin olive oil
- Pepper
- Salt

Instructions. Preheat the oven to 140ºC. Wash and dry basil; peel the garlic. Crush the basil and garlic together with 1 dl of oil. Wash the tomatoes, dry them, and cut them in half lengthwise. Arrange them on the oven plate, brush them with basil oil, and salt pepper, and sprinkle them with a few drops of vinegar. Add the pine nuts and bake for about 1 hour. Peel the onion and cut it into feathers. Clean the salad shoots, wash them and drain them. Dress them with the remaining vinegar, oil, and salt, and stir, so they are impregnated on all sides. Add the pine nuts and onion, and mix well. Place 4 pastry rings on as many plates as possible and fill them with the previous mixture. Arrange the tomatoes on top, carefully remove the rings and serve the salad immediately.

4.11 Zucchini Spaghetti and Sauteed Mushrooms with Scrambled Tofu and Cashew Nuts

Servings: 4

Ingredients

- 400g shiitakes (or other mushrooms)
- 2 courgettes
- 1 purple onion
- 1 clove garlic
- a handful of cashews
- 6-7 stalks of chives
- 4 tablespoons olive oil
- pepper and salt

For the tofu scramble:

- 250 g firm tofu
- 1 tablespoon of tamari
- 1/2 teaspoon smoked paprika
- 1 tablespoon nutritional yeast
- 1 tablespoon of turmeric
- 2 tablespoons olive oil
- sal marina o sal kala namak

Instructions. Take the tofu out of the package, wrap it in a cloth or kitchen paper, put a weight (for example, a cutting board) on top, and let it dry well. Meanwhile, wash the courgettes, trim them, and cut them into spirals with a spiralizer or into thin, elongated strips with the help of a mandolin or a peeler. Blanch the zucchini spirals in boiling salted water for 2 minutes. Drain them and plunge them quickly into a bowl of very cold water. Drain them again and reserve. Peel the onion, cut it into strips and fry them in a large pan with 2 tablespoons of olive oil for about 8-10 minutes over low heat. Add the courgette spirals, salt, and pepper, and sauté for a few moments. Add half of the chopped chives.

4.12 Fennel and Courgette Cream with Vegetable Chips

Servings: 4

Ingredients

- 2 large zucchini
- 1 fennel bulb

- 1 leek
- 1 potato
- 1 liter of water or vegetable broth
- Extra virgin olive oil
- Nutmeg, pepper and salt

For the chips:
- 2 carrots
- 1 beet
- 1/2 yucca
- 1/2 zucchini
- Mild olive oil
- Aromatic herbs or spices
- One of fresh rosemary or the same leaves of the fennel bulb to decorate

Instructions. If you make the chips at home, you must prepare them in advance. You just need to cut the vegetables into very thin slices (2-3 mm), preferably with a mandolin or a vegetable peeler, put them in a large bowl and add olive oil and the spices or aromatic herbs with which you want to season them (for example, curry, dill, paprika, garlic powder, turmeric, cumin, rosemary, thyme...). Mix them well so that they are impregnated. Then you dehydrate them in the dehydrator or, if you don't have one, in the same oven: put it at a temperature of 100-150oC and bake between 30 and 90 minutes, depending on the vegetable. You will have to open the oven occasionally to let the steam out or leave the door ajar and place a wooden spoon across it to prevent it from closing. At the time of making the cream, wash the courgettes well and cut them into pieces. If you want, you can also peel them. Clean the fennel removing the hardest base, and cut it into strips. Peel the potato. Heat a little oil in a large saucepan and fry the leek over low heat until translucent. Stir often with a wooden spoon, so it doesn't burn. Add the courgettes, the fennel, and the potato, leave to sauté slightly with the lid on for a couple of minutes, and cover with the water or vegetable broth. Season with salt and pepper to taste and cook for about 20 minutes, until the vegetables are tender and the potatoes are done. Remove the preparation of leek, fennel, courgette and potato from the heat, crush it and correct salt and pepper. Add a little nutmeg, spread the vegetable chips on top and decorate with the rosemary or some fennel leaves.

4.13 Buckwheat Timbale, Peas, and Tomato with Sprouts

Servings: 4

Ingredients

- 400g buckwheat
- 800 ml of water
- 2 large carrots
- 1 large, very ripe tomato
- 200g peas
- 15 g radish sprouts
- Turmeric
- Oregano
- Peppers
- Extra virgin olive oil
- Pepper
- Salt

Instructions. Cook the buckwheat and let it cool. Peel a carrot and cut it into small dice. Heat a pan with a little olive oil and cook the carrot with the pan covered. After about 15 minutes, or when it is tender, remove and reserve. Repeat the process with the chopped tomato. Cook the peas in salted water for 7 minutes. Reserve 100 g of garnish peas sautéed in a pan with a little olive oil and seasoned. Divide the buckwheat into three equal parts. Blend one part with the tomato, another with the carrot, and the last part with 100 g peas. Add to all a splash of oil and salt and pepper. Season the carrot puree with a little turmeric, the tomato with paprika, and the peas with oregano. Integrate the spices well and reserve. With the help of a stainless steel ring, on a plate, arrange the first layer of the pea mixture, the second of the carrot mixture, and the third of the tomato mixture. Remove the ring. Garnish with the reserved sautéed peas and sprouts.

4.14 Avocado, Zucchini and Chickpea Hummus Served With Crudités

Servings: 6-8

Ingredients

- 2 courgettes chopped
- 8 to 9 tablespoons tahini (preferably raw sesame)
- 1-2 avocados
- 250g chickpeas
- 2 tablespoons nutritional yeast
- 1 lemon, its juice
- 2 cloves of garlic sea salt (to taste)
- water and olive oil if I missed

Instructions. Mix all the ingredients in a blender until you get a homogeneous texture. If it is too thick, add a little water and olive oil until you get the desired texture. Serve this hummus with sticks or sticks, which you can prepare with celery, carrot, cucumber or red pepper. Endives are also very good.

4.15 Salmon papillote with leeks, ginger and teriyaki sauce

Cooking: 10 min **Servings:** 4

Ingredients

- Salmon (clean loins or ingots) 4
- Leek 1
- Carrot two
- Fresh ginger (about 2 cm piece) 1
- teriyaki sauce 60ml
- port wine 60ml
- Star anise 4
- Sesame or sunflower oil 15ml
- ground black pepper

Instructions. We will start by preheating the oven to 180°C. We chop the carrots in julienne, leeks, and ginger. Then we put a pan on the fire with the oil and sauté the vegetables until they are tender. We divide the vegetables into four equal parts and prepare four sheets of baking paper or aluminum foil about 30 by 40 centimeters. We put some of the vegetables, place the salted salmon and cover it with the rest of the vegetables.

4.16 False broccoli couscous with turmeric egg

Cooking: 20 minutes **Servings:** 1

Ingredients

- Small broccoli 1
- Fresh ginger to taste 1
- Small clove of garlic 1
- Sherry vinager 5ml
- Lemon juice 5ml
- Lemon zest (adjust to taste) 1

- Caraway seeds one teaspoon
- Cumin grain one teaspoon
- Dried thyme to taste
- Egg 1
- Two teaspoons of ground turmeric
- Ground black pepper
- Salt
- Extra virgin olive oil

Instructions. Cut the broccoli florets and leaves. Please, do not throw away the trunk; it can be used in creams and soups, steamed al dente, or roasted in the oven with other vegetables. A deliciously tender interior is discovered if the base's woodiest part is cut. Gently wash the florets and leaves, drain and chop with a food processor or chopper. You can also grate or chop roughly with a good knife -and be very careful-. You have to get a very fine grainy texture, like real couscous. Heat a non-stick frying pan and lightly toast the cumin and caraway seeds. Add a little oil with the grated ginger and the minced garlic clove. Stir a few times until they begin to brown, and add the broccoli with the thyme over medium heat. Also, add the large chopped broccoli leaves, reserving the small ones (optional). Sauté for a minute, add the vinegar and lemon juice and stir well. Season and sauté over high heat for a few more minutes. You can leave the texture you want, but it doesn't take long to cook. Keep warm while we cook the egg. Heat a saucepan with plenty of water and one or two heaping teaspoons of turmeric, stirring well to dissolve. Bring to a boil without letting it spurt, and cook the egg by poaching it according to your usual method. The silicone utensils on the market work quite well so as not to get complicated. Take out after 4-8 minutes, depending on how we like it curdled. Serve the false broccoli couscous adjusting the salt level. Top with the freshly made egg and add a pinch of flaky salt and freshly ground black pepper. Accompany with the broccoli leaves that we have reserved, if applicable.

4.17 Low histamine pasta with basil spirulina pesto

Preparation time: 30 min **Serving:** 5

Ingredients
- basil (fresh) - 100 gram
- Spirulina - 30 grams
- pine nuts (roasted) - 40 grams
- rapeseed oil - 50 grams
- olive oil - 50 grams
- Salt - 2 teaspoons / 10g
- young Gouda - 70 grams
- Garlic cloves - 2 pieces / 6 g
- Spelled tagliatelle - 500 grams
- Water - 2 liters / 2000g

Instructions. Heat two liters of water in a large saucepan, salt with 1.5 teaspoons of salt, and add the spelled noodles to the boiling water. Put the lid on and cook the noodles for 8-12 minutes, depending on the package instructions.

Meanwhile, place the pine nuts in a small pan and toast them over medium-high heat until lightly browned. Wash and dry 2 bunches of basil. Peel garlic cloves. Put the pine nuts, basil, garlic cloves, olive oil, rapeseed oil, spirulina powder, and salt in a tall container and mash with a hand blender until you get a creamy pesto. Chop the Gouda as finely as possible with a cheese grater or a knife. Drain the pasta and mix it with the basil and spirulina pesto. Arrange on plates and sprinkle over the Gouda. If you tolerate it and like it, add some pepper.

4.18 Roasted Beet Hummus
Servings: 8
Ingredients
- 1 large red chard
- 2 cups of cooked chickpeas (1 cup dry)
- 4 cloves of garlic
- 2-3 tablespoons of tahini paste
- 1/4 cup of extra virgin olive oil
- 2 tablespoons of lemon juice
- Salt to taste
- Cumin to taste, optional

Instructions. Preheat the oven to 400 ° F. Wash the beetroot and wrap it in foil. Wrap the garlic in foil separately. Place both foil bags in the oven, removing the garlic at 30 minutes and the beetroot at 1 hour. (Beetroot is cooked when you can easily pierce with a fork or knife). Let all ingredients cool completely. Peel the cooked garlic and beetroot and cut the beetroot into quarters. Put the garlic, beetroot pieces, chickpeas, tahini, and lemon juice in a food processor. Puree with 1/4 cup of olive oil. Taste and add a pinch of salt and / or cumin if desired. To serve, collect the hummus in a bowl, drizzle with olive oil and garnish.

4.19 Glazed salmon with miso and sesame salad
Preparation time: 15 minutes + marinade **Cooking time:** 6-8 minutes
Ingredients
For the fish:
- 2 salmon fillets with skin, about 160 g each
- 2 small cloves of garlic, minced
- 2 tablespoons of rice vinegar
- 2 tablespoons of lime juice
- 2 teaspoons of tamari
- 2 teaspoons of white miso
- 2 teaspoons of grated or chopped fresh ginger

For the slaws (you will have the leftovers):
- 1 cup of grated napa or kale
- 3/4 cup watermelon radish, thinly sliced
- 4 small red radishes, thinly sliced
- ½ cup of grated zucchini, carrot
- 1 green onion, diced

- 3 tablespoons chopped cilantro, optional
- avocado, to decorate
- For the sesame dressing:
- juice of 1 large navel orange
- 2 tablespoons of low sodium tamari
- 1 tablespoon of sesame oil, maple syrup, and rice vinegar
- a few pinches of chili flakes, optional

Instructions. Chop all the ingredients for the marinade and place them in a shallow, sealable container. Place the salmon fillets, skin side up, into the marinade. Store in the refrigerator for at least 1 hour. While the fish is marinating, prepare the salad by cutting all the vegetables as directed and whipping the sauce. Pour some dressing over the salad and mix well. When ready to cook, drizzle a large skillet with coconut oil and maximize the heat. After 1 minute, place the fillets skin side up in the pan. Cook for about 5-6 minutes, depending on the thickness of the fish. When the salmon is fully cooked, serve it on 2 plates, topped with a cup or two of coleslaw. Serve the rest in a bowl aside.

4.20 Cauliflower and broccoli salad
Preparation time: 20 min **Cooking time:** 20 min **Servings:**4
Ingredients
- 1 cauliflower
- 1 kg Christmas broccoli (also called white broccoli)
- to taste extra virgin olive oil
- salt to taste
- 1 lemon
- 1 clove of garlic

Instructions. Before preparing the Neapolitan broccoli salad, take the broccoli and clean them. Remove the yellow or dry leaves and the hardest stem, and rinse well with cold water. Apart from cleaning the cauliflower, removing the external green leaves and the stem and cutting it into florets, rinse it. Take 2 large pots, fill them with cold water, add the cauliflower and the broccoli in the other, add salt, put the pots on the stove, and bring them to a boil. Boil both vegetables for 15 minutes from boiling. To check if the broccoli is cooked, take a fork and the same in the pot. If the fork bites well and the broccoli is soft, then it means that the latter is cooked. They must be cooked, same thing for the cauliflower. It will take exactly 15 minutes. Drain both vegetables, add them in a large bowl and let them cool before seasoning them with oil, minced garlic (remove the central core from the garlic), salt, and lemon juice. They are excellent both warm and cold.

4.21 Grilled Salmon with Brussels Sprouts and Pomegranate
Cooking time: 50 minutes **Servings:** 4
Ingredients
- 4 salmon loins
- 1 kilogram of brussels sprout
- 1 pomegranate

- 1 red onion
- 2 cloves of garlic
- 40 milliliters of balsamic vinegar
- 4 tablespoons of olive oil
- Salt

Instructions. Shell the pomegranate: The easiest way is to hit it all over the surface with the back of a spoon. Cut it in half and turn it over on a plate, so the grains fall out; hit it a little more if they stick together. Then, remove the remains of yellow skin that could remain on the grains because it has a bitter taste. **Cut the cabbage:** Put a large saucepan on the fire with plenty of water and a little salt. Cut the base of the cabbage, remove the first leaves and wash them well. Blanch them for a few minutes. Put the cabbages in the water when it starts to boil and blanch them for 4 minutes. After this time, remove them and pass them to a colander to drain well. Keep them warm. **Sauté garlic and onion:** Peel the onion and the garlic cloves, finely chop them and fry them together for 4 minutes in a pan with the oil over medium heat. Add the cabbage. Add the sprouts, pour in 35 ml of balsamic vinegar and cook, covered and occasionally stirring, for about 10 minutes. **Season the salmon:** Check the salmon loins and remove any bones they may have. Wash them well, dry them with a sheet of kitchen paper and splash them on both sides. **Brown the salmon:** Grease a grill with oil, put it on the fire, and, when it is very hot, add the salmon fillets and cook them for 2-3 minutes on each side. Serve with the pomegranate. Arrange the Brussels sprouts on the plates and place the salmon fillets on top. Add the pomegranate grains, decorate with a few threads of the remaining balsamic vinegar, and serve hot immediately.

4.22 Turkey Burgers with Tzatziki Sauce

Preparation time: 22 Minutes **Cooking time:** 20 Minutes **Serving:** 4 Persons

Ingredients

- 1/2 cup fresh parsley (chopped)
- 1 pound ground turkey
- 3/4 cup bread crumbs
- 1 egg
- 1 sweet onion (minced)
- 2 garlic cloves (minced)
- 1/4 teaspoon red-pepper flakes
- 1 tablespoon extra-virgin olive oil
- 1/2 teaspoon dried oregano
- Salt
- Freshly ground black pepper

Tzatziki Sauce:

- 1 cup Greek yogurt

- 1/2 European cucumber (diced)
- 1/4 cup fresh parsley (chopped)
- 1 tablespoon extra-virgin olive oil
- 2 tablespoons lemon juice
- 1 pinch of garlic powder
- Salt
- Freshly ground black pepper

Toppings:

- 1/2 red onion (sliced)
- 4 hamburger buns (whole-wheat)
- 8 Boston lettuce leaves
- 2 tomatoes (sliced)

Instructions. Burgers: Put the oil in a pan and heat it over medium heat. For around 4 minutes, saute the onion. Add the garlic. Maintain the low heat for one more minute of sauteing. Putting aside. Combine the turkey, oregano, pepper flakes, parsley, cooled onion, and egg in a large mixing basin. Combine in a harmonious manner. Add the bread crumbs, seasoning, and pepper. Combine in a harmonious manner. Turn the oven temperature up to 350 degrees F. Make 4 burgers out of the turkey mixture. Put some cooking spray in a skillet that can go from the stovetop to the oven and heat it over medium. Place the burger inside. Brown the meat by searing it for 5 minutes on each side. You should bake the skillet. The burgers need to be baked for 17 minutes. **Tzatziki Sauce:** Put the garlic powder, olive oil, lime juice, yogurt, and cucumber in a bowl and stir well. Combine in a harmonious manner. You may add salt and pepper to taste. The parsley should be added now.

Nutrition Calories: 350 Kcal, Proteins: 54g, Fat: 7g, Carbohydrates: 10g

4.23 Fried Rice with Pineapple

Preparation time: 10 Minutes **Cooking time:** 15 Minutes **Serving:** 3 Persons

Ingredients

- 1/2 cup frozen corn
- 3 cups brown rice (cooked)
- 2 cups pineapple (diced)
- 1/2 cup ham (diced)
- 1/2 cup frozen peas
- 3 tablespoons soy sauce
- 1 tablespoon sesame oil
- 2 tablespoons olive oil
- 2 green onions (sliced)

- 1 onion (diced)
- 2 carrots (peeled and grated)
- 2 cloves garlic (minced)
- 1/2 teaspoon ginger powder
- 1/4 teaspoon white pepper

Instructions. Combine the soy sauce, sesame oil, ginger powder, and white ginger powder in a bowl. Combine in a harmonious manner. The olive oil should be heated in a pan over medium heat. For around 4 minutes, sauté the onion and garlic.

Coat the pan with oil and add the vegetables. Prepare in 4 minutes. Add the rice, pineapple, ham, green onions, and soy sauce mixture to the pan. Continue stirring for a few minutes as the food cooks. Serve. **Nutrition** Calories: 179 Kcal, Proteins: 3g, Fat: 5g, Carbohydrates: 30g

4.24 Ratatouille

Preparation time: 10 Minutes **Cooking time:** 15 Minutes **Serving:** 5 Persons

Ingredients

- 1 medium red onion (thickly sliced)
- 1 small eggplant
- 1 cup tomato sauce
- 2 small red bell peppers (halved)
- 2 medium summer squash
- Salt
- 2 medium zucchini
- 3 medium tomatoes
- 2 sprigs oregano
- 2 garlic cloves (smashed)
- Freshly ground black pepper
- 2 tablespoons thyme leaves
- 5 tablespoons olive oil

Instructions. Turn the oven temperature up to 375 degrees F. Prepare a baking tray for four individual plates. Put the oil in a saucepan and heat it over medium heat. Garlic should be cooked for a minute in a skillet. Shut off the furnace. Mix in the oregano. Wait 15 minutes and strain. Throw out the oregano and garlic. Put 2 tablespoons of the oil into each individual baking dish. Apply a little amount of tomato sauce to the bottom of each baking tray. Distribute the eggplant, squash, onion, zucchini, tomato, and bell pepper evenly among the baking dishes. Slices should be closely packed and slightly staggered. Add the remaining tomato sauce and spread it out. Use the leftover olive oil as a finishing touch. Add thyme, pepper, and salt to taste. Do a 30-minute roast. Give it a few minutes to cool off. Serve.

Nutrition Calories: 127 Kcal, Proteins: 2.1g, Fat: 7.1g, Carbohydrates: 16g

4.25 Eggs with Tomatoes and Asparagus

Preparation time: 10 Minutes **Cooking time:** 10 Minutes **Serving:** 4 Persons

Ingredients

- 2 pounds asparagus
- 1-pint cherry tomatoes
- 4 eggs
- Salt
- 2 tablespoons olive oil
- 2 teaspoons fresh thyme (chopped)
- Pepper

Instructions. Turn the oven temperature up to 400 degrees F. Spray some cooking spray in a baking dish. Arrange a single layer of tomato halves and asparagus spears on the oiled baking sheet. Spread the olive oil throughout. Spice it up with salt, pepper, and thyme. Cook at 400° for 12 minutes. Take it out of the oven. Make an omelet with the asparagus and the eggs. Add salt and pepper to taste. Put the dish in the oven and set the timer for 7 minutes. Serve. **Nutrition** Calories: 290 Kcal, Proteins: 13g, Fat: 17g, Carbohydrates: 21g

4.26 Turmeric, Carrot, and Ginger Soup

Preparation time: 10 Minutes **Cooking time:** 10 Minutes **Serving:** 4 Persons

Ingredients

- 3 carrots (diced)
- 4 cups vegetable stock
- Canned coconut milk (for topping)
- 3 cloves garlic (minced)
- 1-inch fresh ginger (finely grated)
- 2 inches of fresh turmeric (finely grated)
- 1 white onion (diced)
- Black sesame seeds (for topping)
- 1 tablespoon lemon juice

Instructions. Put some olive oil in a saucepan and cook it over medium heat. Caramelize the onion in a skillet. Prepare the dish by adding the spices. Keep cooking for another minute. Prepare by adding carrots. To prepare, you will need to spend two minutes cooking. Incorporate the vegetable stock. Maintain a low boil for 25 minutes. Use a stick blender to purée the soup. Prepare the dish by adding lemon juice. Stir. To serve, stir with some coconut milk and sprinkle with black sesame seeds.

Nutrition Calories: 103 Kcal, Proteins: 2g, Fat: 3g, Carbohydrates: 18g

4.27 Bulgur and Sweet Potato Salad

Preparation time: 15 Minutes **Cooking time:** 40 Minutes **Serving:** 4 Persons

Ingredients

- 1 1/4 cups bulgur wheat
- 2 medium sweet potatoes
- 1 cup parsley (finely chopped)
- 1/4 cup olive oil
- 1/2 cup mint (finely chopped)
- 1/4 cup red onion (finely chopped)
- 2 tablespoons orange zest
- 1/4 cup orange juice (freshly squeezed)
- 2 tablespoons lemon juice
- 1 tablespoon avocado oil
- 1 tablespoon red wine vinegar
- 2 teaspoons maple syrup
- 1 small clove of garlic (grated)
- 1/2 teaspoon salt
- Coarse salt
- Freshly ground black pepper
- Black pepper

Instructions. Turn on the oven to 450 degrees Fahrenheit. Prepare parchment paper on a baking pan. The sweet potatoes, maple syrup, and avocado oil should be combined in a bowl. Add salt and pepper to taste. Combine by tossing. Evenly disperse on the prepared baking sheet. Set the timer for 40 minutes and roast. Toss during the midway point of roasting. Bring 3 and a half cups of water to a boil in a saucepan set over medium heat. Start a boil with this. Add the bulgur to the pot. Stir. Turn down the stove. Stirring occasionally, let simmer for 8 minutes. Shut off the furnace. Put the lid on it. Keep quiet for 10 minutes. Get rid of the fluid. Gently stir the bulgur. Combine the garlic, pepper, vinegar, salt, citrus juices, olive oil, and orange juice in a bowl. Combine everything well. Combine the vinegar and garlic in a separate bowl; add the bulgur, parsley, mint, orange zest, and red onion. Combine by tossing. Serve.

Nutrition Calories: 103 Kcal, Proteins: 2g, Fat: 3g, Carbohydrates: 18g

4.28 Salmon Roast with Romaine and Potatoes

Preparation time: 15 Minutes **Cooking time:** 30 Minutes **Serving:** 4 Persons

Ingredients

- 2 hearts of romaine lettuce (cut in half)
- 1 pound of baby potatoes (rinsed)

- 4 (6-ounce) salmon fillets
- 1 tablespoon butter (melted)
- 4 tablespoons olive oil (divided)
- 1 teaspoon lemon juice
- Freshly ground black pepper
- 1/4 teaspoon paprika
- Salt

Instructions. Turn on the oven to 450 degrees F. Put some cooking spray on a baking sheet. Place the remaining potatoes and olive oil in a bowl. Place on coat and toss. Put the potatoes in a single layer on a baking sheet that has been oiled. Roast for twenty minutes at 400°. Combine the remaining olive oil and the lime juice, and rub it into the romaine lettuce. Put some salt and pepper on it. The fillets of salmon should be brushed with melted butter. Sprinkle with salt, pepper, and paprika. Salmon fillets, romaine lettuce, and potatoes should all be spread out on a baking pan. Repeat the roasting process for 7 more minutes. Serve.

Nutrition Calories: 147 Kcal, Proteins: 0g, Fat: 4g, Carbohydrates: 1g

4.29 Bean Bolognese
Preparation time: 15 Minutes **Cooking time:** 30 Minutes **Serving:** 4 Persons

Ingredients

- 1 can (14-ounce) white beans
- 2 carrots
- 1 onion
- 1 can (28-ounce) crushed tomatoes
- 2 cloves garlic
- 2 celery stalks

Instructions. Put everything into a slow cooker. Put it in the oven and let it there for 6 hours.

Nutrition Calories: 442 Kcal, Proteins: 17g, Fat: 11g, Carbohydrates: 68g

4.30 Peppers Stuffed with Sweet Potato and Turkey
Preparation time: 15 Minutes **Cooking time:** 20 Minutes **Serving:** 4 Persons

Ingredients

- 1 2/3 cups sweet potatoes (diced)
- 2 cups ground turkey
- 1/2 cup tomato sauce
- 2 large bell peppers (cut in half)
- 1/2 cup onions (diced)

- 1 tablespoon extra-virgin olive oil

- Pepper

- 2 cloves garlic (minced)

- Fresh parsley (for garnishing)

- Salt

Instructions. Get the oven ready at 350 degrees. Spray some cooking spray on a baking sheet. Olive oil should be heated in a pan over medium heat. Add the turkey and garlic. Break up the meat while it cooks and let it simmer for 10 minutes while being stirred occasionally. Toss the onions in. You just need 5 minutes to cook. Combine the potatoes into the mixture. Cover. Maintain a simmer for 8 minutes, stirring occasionally. Mix in the salt, pepper, and tomato sauce. Put the peppers in a single layer on a prepared baking sheet. Here, the opening is pointing upwards. Stuff the sweet potato and turkey mixture into the bell peppers until they are almost full. Put in the oven and set the timer for 30 minutes. Dress with chopped parsley. Serve.

Nutrition Calories: 324 Kcal, Proteins: 25g, Fat: 13g, Carbohydrates: 26g

4.31 Turkey Meatballs

Preparation time: 10 Minutes **Cooking time:** 30 Minutes **Serving:** 4 Persons

Ingredients

- 1/2 cup fresh Parmesan cheese (grated)

- 1 pound ground turkey

- 1/2 cup fresh breadcrumbs (whole wheat)

- 2-3 tablespoons of water

- 1 large egg (beaten)

- 1 tablespoon fresh parsley (chopped)

- 1/2 tablespoon fresh basil (chopped)

- 1/2 tablespoon fresh oregano (chopped)

- Pinch of fresh nutmeg (grated)

Instructions. Get the oven ready at 350 degrees. Put parchment paper on two baking sheets. Mix the turkey, breadcrumbs, cheese, egg, water, herbs, nutmeg, salt, and pepper in a large bowl. Combine everything well. If the combination is too dry to form a ball, add a little more water. Roll the dough into 30 little balls. Put the balls in a neat row on the prepared baking sheets. Put in the oven and set the timer for 30 minutes. To ensure even baking, flip the balls midway through the cooking time. Serve.

Nutrition Calories: 140 Kcal, Proteins: 14g, Fat: 9g, Carbohydrates: 5g

4.32 Ramen

Serving: 2

Ingredients

For the broth:

- 3 whole chicken breasts with skin
- 2 carrots cut into large pieces
- 1/4 onion
- 2 finely chopped spring onions
- 1 piece fresh ginger root
- 1.5 liter water

For the plate:

- 1 zucchini
- 1/2 sliced chicken breast (from the broth)
- Fresh coriander
- Shitake mushrooms
- 1 spring onion (the green part)
- 2 boiled eggs
- Tamari sauce

Instructions. Put all the ingredients of the broth in a pot and put it on high heat. When it starts to boil, lower the heat to a simmer and leave for about 1 hour and a half. Strain the broth and remove the breasts. Slice half a breast for each bowl. (The rest you can keep in the fridge to prepare other dishes). Spirilize the zucchini with a specialized machine. Pour the chicken broth over the zucchini spaghetti to cover. Then place the sliced chicken, the mushrooms, the spring onion and the egg. **Notes:** I recommend eating it with chopsticks and when it is very hot.

4.33 Gluten or sugar free pancakes

Servings: 2

Ingredients

- 1 + 1/2 cup vanilla oatmeal powder
- 250ml milk
- 2 very ripe bananas
- 1/2 cup yeast
- 1 Medjoul woodpecker
- 1 pinch salt
- 2 tsp chia seeds
- 1/4 tsp ground cinnamon
- 1/2 cup fresh blueberries
- 2 tbsp fresh cheese
- 2 tbsp plain yogurt
- Hazelnut cream
- fruit of the passion

Instructions. Put the oats, the milk, the bananas, the yeast, the dates, the salt, the seeds and the cinnamon in the blender glass or the processor and blend until you get a homogeneous mass. Let stand about 10 minutes. Meanwhile, mix the fresh cheese and yogurt in a bowl. Add a few drops of olive oil to a non-stick pan and spread over the entire surface with the help of a brush. Fill a ladle with the batter and pour it into the pan. When you see that little bubbles start to come out and the color of the pancake darkens, it's time to turn it over. It usually takes about a minute on each side (when we start to see bubbles in the dough, it's time to turn it over). If the pan is large, several can be made simultaneously. When you have made all the pancakes, make the tower alternating a pancake, a little hazelnut cream, a little cheese and yogurt mixture, and another little passion fruit. Finally, decorate with a handful of fresh blueberries.

4.34 Omelette with eggs, cabbage, and turmeric
Ingredients
- 2 eggs
- 1 chopped cabbage
- 1 and a half teaspoons of turmeric
- Garlic
- 1 teaspoon of butter
- Salt and Pepper To Taste

Instructions. Heat the butter in a skillet. In a bowl he beat the eggs. Add chopped cabbage to the pan, a clove of garlic and cook until it becomes slightly wilted. Then add the beaten eggs, turmeric, salt and pepper. Finally, serve with toast if you like.

4.35 Bone broth
Ingredients
- chicken, hen, beef, pork bones
- carrot in pieces
- 1 rama tomillo fresco
- 1 onion cut into pieces
- agua
- salt

Instructions. Add all the ingredients to a pressure cooker or a conventional pot. If you use a conventional pot, boil over medium-low heat slowly for a minimum of 24 hours, but you can do it for up to 72 hours. If you use a pressure cooker, reduce the time by half, as cooking is faster. At the end of cooking, remove from heat and let stand until cool. Remove the bones and clean the broth from the vegetables. If you wish, pass the broth through a mesh to clean it of some remaining impurities after the process. Store in the freezer or the fridge, depending on how often you use it.

4.36 Red onions stuffed with couscous and apricots

Preparation: 20 min **Ready in:** 50 min **Calories:** 266 kcal **Servings:** 4

Ingredients

- 350ml _ vegetable broth
- 125g _ couscous
- 8th red onions
- 10g _ coriander (0.5 bunch)
- 10g _ parsley (0.5 bunch)
- 100g _ dried apricots
- 2 garlic cloves
- 2 tbsp olive oil
- 1 pinch organic lemon zest
- iodized salt with fluoride
- Pepper
- ½ tsp ground cumin

Instructions. Bring 250 ml of broth to a boil, pour over the couscous and leave covered for 15 minutes. Meanwhile, cut off a cap from each onion. Hollow out the onions, leaving a wall at least 1/2 cm thick; roughly chop the core of the onion. Wash herbs, shake dry, and chop finely. Cut apricots into small pieces. Peel and chop the garlic. Heat oil in a pan. Sauté chopped onions and garlic for 2 minutes over medium heat. Add apricots, herbs, and couscous, mix everything, and season with lemon zest, salt, pepper, and cumin. Salt the inside of the hollowed-out onions, add the couscous mixture, and press down lightly. Place the onions in a casserole dish and put the hats on. Pour in the rest of the broth and cook everything in a preheated oven at 200 °C (convection: 180 °C; gas: level 3) for 30 minutes.

4.37 Chard and broccoli salad with buttermilk dressing

Preparation: 30 min **Calories:** 197 kcal **Servings:** 4

Ingredients

- 50g _ sunflower seeds
- 300g _ broccoli (0.5 broccoli)
- iodized salt with fluoride
- 200g _ young chard (1 perennial)
- 2 stems mint
- 250g _ large red apples (1 large red apple)
- ½ lemon (juice)
- 100ml _ buttermilk
- 40g _ yoghurt (1.5% fat) (2 tbsp)
- 1 tbsp apple cider vinegar
- 1 tsp hot mustard
- Pepper
- 3 tsp olive oil
- 1 tsp honey

Instructions. Roast the sunflower seeds in a hot pan without fat over medium heat for 3 minutes; put aside. Clean the broccoli, wash, divide it into small florets and cook in boiling salted water for about 2 minutes; then rinse and drain. Clean and wash the chard, remove the coarse stalks, cut the leaves into fine strips and cook in boiling salted water for 3–4 minutes; drain and drain. Wash the mint, shake it dry and pluck off the leaves. Wash the apple, quarter, core, cut into fine sticks and mix with the lemon juice. Whisk together the buttermilk, yogurt, vinegar, mustard, salt, pepper, oil, and honey. Mix the chard strips, broccoli, apple and 2/3 of the mint and spread on plates. Pour the buttermilk dressing, sprinkle over the sunflower seeds and garnish the salad with the remaining mint leaves.

4.38 Sesame-crusted salmon and broccoli

Preparation: 25 mins **Calories:** 406 kcal **Servings:** 4

Ingredients

- 600g _ broccoli
- iodized salt with fluoride
- 1 clove of garlic
- 15g _ginger
- 480g _ very fresh salmon fillet (8 pieces)
- pepper
- 30g _ sesame
- 15g _ coconut oil (1 tbsp)
- 2 tbsp sesame oil
- chili thread
- 50ml _ vegetable broth
- 2 tbsp lime juice
- 1 lime

Instructions. Clean and wash the broccoli and cut it into florets. Cook in boiling salted water for 4 minutes, drain, rinse and drain well. Meanwhile, peel and finely chop the garlic. Peel and finely grate the ginger. Rinse the salmon under cold water, pat dry, season with salt and pepper, and coat with sesame seeds. Heat coconut oil in a pan and fry the salmon on the skin side until golden brown. Then flip and fry on the other side until golden brown. Place on an ovenproof plate or a baking tray and stand in a preheated oven at 100 °C (convection oven not recommended; gas: lowest setting) for approx. 10 minutes (it should still be translucent on the inside). Meanwhile, heat sesame oil in a wok and sauté garlic and ginger. Add broccoli and chili threads, mix in, deglaze with broth, and season with salt, pepper, and lime juice. Rinse the lime in hot water, pat dry, and cut into wedges. Place 2 pieces of salmon and the broccoli on 4 plates and garnish with lime wedges.

4.39 Fennel salad with grapefruit

Preparation: 25 mins **Calories:** 236 kcal **Servings:** 4

Ingredients

- 4 tubers
- fennel
- 2 grapefruits
- 4 tbsp sesame oil
- 1 pinch raw cane sugar
- 2 tbsp red wine vinegar
- salt
- pepper
- chili flakes
- 30g _ walnuts

Kitchen appliances. 1 knife, 1 salad bowl, 1 coated pan

Instructions. Wash the fennel thoroughly, cut it in half, de-stem, and put the fennel greens aside. Cut or slice the fennel into fine strips and place in a bowl. Thoroughly peel the grapefruits with a knife. Cut out the pulp between the membranes; Cut the fillets into pieces and set aside. Squeeze the remaining grapefruit and add the juice to the fennel. Add the sesame oil, raw cane sugar, and red wine vinegar to the fennel and season with salt, pepper, and chili flakes. Knead everything vigorously with your hands. Add grapefruit and let steep for 10 minutes. Meanwhile, toast the walnuts in a pan without fat over medium heat; remove and roughly chop. Roughly chop the green fennel as well. Pour the fennel salad into four bowls and top with the fennel greens and walnuts.

4.40 Carrot tagliatelle with avocado pesto

Preparation: 30 min **Calories:** 237 kcal **Servings:** 4

Ingredients

- 30g _ pine nuts (2 tbsp)
- 1 ripe avocado
- 2 tbsp lime juice
- Salt

- Pepper
- 1 pinch chili flakes
- 800g _ long carrots (8 long carrots)
- 80g _ rocket (1 bunch)
- 3 stems oregano
- 2 tbsp olive oil
- 75ml _ vegetable broth
- 250g _ cherry tomatoes

Instructions. Roast the pine nuts in a hot pan without oil over medium heat for 3 minutes. Halve the avocado, remove the stone, scoop the flesh out of the skin with a spoon, and place it in a tall mug. Add half of the pine nuts and the lime juice and puree everything finely. Season to taste with salt, pepper, and chili flakes. Clean and peel the carrots and cut them into long, narrow strips (tagliatelle) using a vegetable peeler. Wash oregano, shake dry, and pluck off the leaves. Heat oil in a large pan. Fry the carrot tagliatelle in it over medium heat for 4 minutes. Deglaze with broth and simmer over low heat for 5 minutes, occasionally turning, until the liquid has evaporated. Meanwhile, clean, wash and quarter the cherry tomatoes. Season the carrot tagliatelle with salt and pepper. Add tomatoes and sauté for 2 minutes. Serve the carrot tagliatelle with the avocado pesto and sprinkle with pine nuts and oregano leaves.

4.41 Vegetable quinoa bowl with peanut dip
Preparation: 35 min **Calories:** 339 kcal **Servings:** 2
Ingredients
- 100g _ quinoa
- 1 tsp turmeric powder
- Salt
- 300g _ celeriac (0.5 celeriac)
- 1 carrot
- 1 tsp olive oil
- Pepper
- Paprika powder
- Dried marjoram
- Dried thyme
- 2 stems parsley
- 100g _ yoghurt (3.5% fat)
- 1 tbsp peanut butter
- 1 pinch chili flakes
- 15g _ peanut kernel (1 tbsp)
- 50g _ baby spinach
- 30g _ pomegranate seeds (2 tbsp)

Instructions. Rinse the quinoa, drain and cook with the turmeric and twice the amount of boiling salted water for 15 minutes, then remove from the heat and leave to soak. Meanwhile, peel the celery and carrot and cut them into small cubes.

Heat the oil in a pan and sauté the diced vegetables over medium heat for about 10 minutes, stirring occasionally. Season with salt, pepper, and spices. Wash the parsley, shake it dry and chop it finely. Mix the yogurt with the peanut butter and half the parsley, and season with salt, pepper, and chili flakes. Chop peanuts. Place the quinoa in two bowls with the spinach, arrange the vegetables on top, drizzle the sauce over them, and sprinkle with the nuts, the remaining parsley, and the pomegranate seeds.

4.42 Salmon on tomato and fennel vegetables

Preparation: 25 min **Calories:** 563 kcal **Servings:** 2

Ingredients

- 1 red onion
- 2 tubers fennel
- 2 tomatoes
- 2 branches
- Thyme
- 30g _ walnut kernels (2 tbsp)
- 4 tbsp olive oil
- Salt
- Pepper
- Cayenne pepper
- 250g _ salmon fillet (2 salmon fillets)
- ½ tsp herbs of Provence

Instructions. Peel the onion, halve and cut it into strips. Clean the fennel, wash, cut out the stalk, halve, and cut into strips. Clean, wash and chop the tomatoes. Wash the thyme, shake it dry and pluck off the leaves. Roughly chop the walnut kernels. Heat 2 tablespoons of oil in a pan and sauté onion strips with the fennel for 5 minutes over medium heat. Add the nuts and tomatoes, and sauté briefly for another 5 minutes; pour in 2 tablespoons of water and stew, covered, for about 5 minutes over low heat. Season to taste with salt, pepper, thyme, and cayenne pepper. Rinse the salmon fillets, pat dry, and season with salt. Heat the remaining oil in a pan, fry the salmon fillets for 3 minutes on each side over medium heat, and season with herbs de Provence, salt, and pepper. Serve the salmon fillet on the vegetables.

4.43 Zucchini noodles with wild garlic pesto

Working time: 15 min **Completed in:** 30 min **Calories:** 578 **Servings:** 2

Ingredients

- Zucchini/s 3 pieces / 600g
- Cherry tomatoes 10 pieces / 120g
- Pine nuts 50 grams
- Wild garlic 150 grams
- Sea-salt ½ teaspoon / 2½ g
- Cashews 80 grams
- Olive oil (virgin) 3 tablespoons / 25g

Instructions. Soak the cashews in water overnight or simmer them in the pot for 15 minutes. Wash the zucchini and use a spiralizer to cut them into zoodles for the zucchini noodles. Place zucchini noodles in a colander and rinse with hot water for a few seconds. Wash and halve the cherry tomatoes. For the wild garlic pesto, use a hand blender to puree the soaked cashews with wild garlic, salt, olive oil, and lemon juice to form a pesto. Add a little more olive oil if needed. Serve the zucchini noodles with fresh wild garlic pesto, cherry tomatoes, and pine nuts.

4.44 Arugula, quinoa and goat cheese salad

Preparation: 25 min **Calories:** 593 kcal **Servings:** 4

Ingredients

- 300g _ quinoa
- Salt
- 150g _ rocket (2 bunches)
- 100g _ hazelnut kernels
- 140g _ firm goat cheese
- 2 tbsp lemon juice
- 4 tbsp mild olive oil
- pepper
- 4 tsp liquid honey

Instructions. Rinse the quinoa in a colander under hot water until it runs clear. Place in a saucepan and cook in salted water according to package directions. In the meantime, wash and dry the arugula. Roughly chop the hazelnuts. Crumble the goat cheese. Mix quinoa with lemon juice and olive oil and season with salt and pepper. Mix the quinoa, rocket, hazelnuts, and goat's cheese on 4 plates and drizzle with 1 teaspoon of honey.

4.45 Cauliflower Rice and Salmon Bowl

Preparation time: 15 Minutes **Cooking time:** 20 Minutes **Serving:** 4 Persons

Ingredients

- 1/2 head cauliflower (riced)
- 2 salmon fillets
- 1 bunch kale (shredded)
- 1 teaspoon curry powder
- 3 tablespoons olive oil
- 12 Brussels sprouts (halved)
- Himalayan salt

Marinade:

- 1 tablespoon sesame seeds
- 1/4 cup tamari sauce
- 1 teaspoon Dijon mustard

- 1 teaspoon sesame oil
- 1 teaspoon maple syrup

Instructions. Get the oven ready at 350 degrees. Prepare parchment paper on a baking pan. The Brussels sprouts should be placed on the prepared baking sheet. Put a spoonful of olive oil on it and coat it well. Prepare by adding salt. Cook at 400° for 20 minutes. Combine the marinade's components in a basin. Combine everything well. Substitute the salmon fillets for the Brussels sprouts on the baking pan. Sprinkle the marinade over the fillets. Put in the oven for 15 minutes. Place a teaspoon of olive oil in a saucepan and heat it over medium heat. For three minutes, sauté the kale. Put aside for the time being. Turn the heat to medium and add the remaining olive oil to the same pan. The curry powder, cauliflower rice, and salt should be added now. Stir-fry for three minutes. Split the salmon and brussels sprouts between two plates. To finish, sprinkle some kale and cauliflower rice over the top. Serve.

4.46 Harissa and Chicken Tenders

Preparation time: 15 Minutes **Cooking time:** 15 Minutes **Serving:** 6 Persons

Ingredients

- 1/4 cup plain Greek yogurt
- 2 tablespoons harissa paste
- 24 pieces of chicken tenders
- 1/4 cup dry white wine

Instructions. Place the yogurt, wine, and harissa in a bowl. Combine everything well. Chicken tenders should be inserted. Apply the marinade to the tenders. Cover. Put the marinade into the fridge and let it sit for at least two hours. Grills should be preheated. The chicken strips need to be drained. Allow any surplus liquid to drain. Cook the tenders on the grill for 5 minutes total. You may make a sandwich out of the tenders. Add your favorite fresh herbs and sliced vegetables on top.

Nutrition Calories: 800 Kcal, Proteins: 51g, Fat: 37g, Carbohydrates: 62g

4.47 Chinese Chicken Salad

Preparation time: 15 Minutes **Cooking time:** 10 Minutes **Serving:** 4 Persons

Ingredients

Dressing:
- 1/4-inch ginger (peeled and chopped)
- 1/2 cup vegetable oil
- 1/4 cup rice wine vinegar (unseasoned)
- 1 tablespoon Dijon mustard
- 1 tablespoon soy sauce (low-sodium)
- 2 garlic cloves (minced)
- Pinch of salt

- 1 teaspoon sesame oil

Salad:

- 1/4 cup cooked edamame
- 4 cups green cabbage (shredded)
- 1 cup red cabbage (shredded)
- 2 cooked chicken breasts (shredded)
- 1/2 cup cilantro leaves (chopped)
- 1 small carrot (thin strips)
- 2 tablespoons mint leaves (chopped)
- 4 scallions (thinly sliced)
- Wonton strips

Instructions. All the dressing components should be placed in a blender and blended together. Combine in a blender and blend until smooth. Put everything that will go into the salad into a large mixing bowl. Dress the salad and serve. Put everything in a bowl and shake it up. Add wonton strips as a garnish. Serve.

4.48 Baked Cauliflower Buffalo

Preparation time: 15 Minutes **Cooking time:** 10 Minutes **Serving:** 4 Persons

Ingredients

- 1/4 cup water
- 1/2 cup hot sauce
- 1/4 cup banana flour
- 2 tablespoons butter (melted)
- 1 medium cauliflower (bite-sized)
- Pinch of pepper
- Ranch dressing (for serving)
- Pinch of salt

Instructions. First, set the oven temperature to 425 degrees F. Cover a baking tray with foil. Water, pepper, flour, and salt should be combined in a bowl. Combine everything well. Cauliflower should be included. Mix well by tossing. Arrange the coated cauliflower in an even layer on the prepared baking sheet. Put in the oven for fifteen min. Midway during cooking time, turn the cauliflower over. The butter and spicy sauce should be combined in a separate bowl. Combine everything well. Coat the cauliflower with the sauce. Add another 20 minutes of baking time. Toss with ranch dressing and serve.

4.49 Kale and Sweet Potato Tostadas

Preparation time: 15 Minutes **Cooking time:** 10 Minutes **Serving:** 4 Persons

Ingredients

- 2 medium sweet potatoes (cleaned and chopped)
- 8 stems of kale (roughly chopped)
- 12 Brussels sprouts (finely chopped)
- 1 tablespoon lime juice
- 2 tablespoons olive oil
- 1 tablespoon olive oil
- Pinch of salt
- 1 teaspoon honey
- Corn tortillas
- Pinch of cayenne pepper
- Toasted coconut
- Fresh mint (chopped)
- Yogurt

Instructions. Turn the oven temperature up to 400 degrees F. Using foil, effective style baking sheets. The sweet potatoes should be placed on a baking pan that has been lined. Use olive oil as a finishing touch. Spike it up with some cayenne pepper. Just toss it on the coat. The greens should go on the second baking sheet that has been prepared in the same way. Dress with a drizzle of olive oil. Prepare by adding salt. Just toss it on the coat. Fire up the oven with both baking trays inside. For just around 10 minutes, the kale may be roasted. For Forty minutes, roast the sweet potatoes. Combine the Brussels sprouts, honey, and lime juice in a bowl. Mix well by tossing. Corn tortillas may be piled high on a sheet of aluminum foil. Put it in a preheated 3-minute toasting cycle in the oven. Wrap the sweet potato and greens in a tortilla. Sprinkle some toasted coconut, mint, yogurt, and Brussels sprouts on top. Serve.

CHAPTER 5: Anti-Inflammatory Snack Recipes

5.1 Spicy Tuna Rolls

Preparation time: 15 Minutes **Cooking time:** 10 Minutes **Serving:** 4 Persons

Ingredients

- 1 medium cucumber
- 1 pouch Yellowfin Tuna
- 1/16 teaspoon ground cayenne
- 2 avocado slices (cut into 6 pieces in total)
- 1/8 teaspoon pepper
- 1 teaspoon hot sauce
- 1/8 teaspoon salt

Instructions. Cut the cucumber into thin, long slices. Cucumbers used for slicing must be seedless. Generate a total of six servings. Roll the slices in paper towels to dry them. Combine the tuna, pepper, cayenne, salt, and spicy sauce in a bowl. Combine everything well. Top the cucumber rounds with the tuna spread. Avoid crowding the edges. The dish would benefit from one avocado slice. Carefully roll the cucumber. Insert toothpicks into each roll to keep it together. Serve.

Nutrition Calories: 190 Kcal, Proteins: 6g, Fat: 6g, Carbohydrates: 24g

5.2 Turmeric Gummies

Preparation time: 15 Minutes **Cooking time:** 20 Minutes **Serving:** 6 Persons

Ingredients

- 8 tablespoons gelatin powder (unflavored)
- 3 1/2 cups of water
- 6 tablespoons maple syrup
- Pinch of ground pepper
- 1 teaspoon ground turmeric

Instructions. Combine the water, turmeric, and maple syrup in a saucepan and boil over medium. Stir constantly and let cook for 5 minutes. Shut off the furnace. Blend with some gelatin powder. Combine everything well. Bring the temperature up to maximum. In order to mix the gelatin powder, stir the contents of the saucepan vigorously. Fill molds made of silicon with the mixture. Cover. Put in the refrigerator and chill for at least four hours. Cut them up into manageable gummy chunks. Serve.

Nutrition Calories: 22 Kcal, Proteins: 0g, Fat: 0g, Carbohydrates: 5.2g

5.3 Ginger-Cinnamon Mixed Nuts

Preparation time: 10 Minutes **Cooking time:** 15 Minutes **Serving:** 4 Persons

Ingredients

- 2 large egg whites
- Coconut oil spray
- 2 cups mixed nuts
- 1 teaspoon fresh ginger (grated)
- 1/2 teaspoon fine sea salt
- 1/2 teaspoon ground Vietnamese cinnamon

Instructions. Get the oven ready at 250 degrees F. Place the egg whites in a large mixing dish. Mix with a mixer until foamy. Mix in the salt, ginger, and cinnamon. Combine all of the ingredients by whipping them together. Add the roasted and salted mixed nuts. The coating may be achieved with a good mix. Spray coconut oil onto a sheet of parchment paper. Prepare a baking sheet with parchment paper. Create a flat layer of nuts on the baking sheet. Put it in the oven and set the timer for 40 minutes. Halfway through, flip the baking sheet. It's best to wait until the nuts have cooled and hardened. Split them apart and use the pieces in various ways.

Nutrition Calories: 173 Kcal, Proteins: 5g, Fat: 16g, Carbohydrates: 6g

5.4 Ginger Date Almond Bars

Preparation time: 5 Minutes **Cooking time:** 15 Minutes **Serving:** 4 Persons

Ingredients

- 1 teaspoon ground ginger
- 1/4 cup almond milk
- 1 cup almond flour
- 3/4 cup dates

Instructions. Get the oven ready at 350 degrees. Mix the dates and almond milk in a blender. Put everything in a blender and whir it for 5 minutes until it becomes a paste. Add the ground almonds and ginger. Put in other ingredients and blend for three more minutes. Place the ingredients in a casserole. Hold off till it cools. Break up into eight bars. Serve.

Nutrition Calories: 270 Kcal, Proteins: 10g, Fat: 16g, Carbohydrates: 24g

5.5 Coffee Cacao Protein Bars

Preparation time: 5 Minutes **Cooking time:** 20 Minutes **Serving:** 8 Persons

Ingredients

- 18 large Medjool dates (pitted)
- 2 cups mixed nuts
- 1 cup egg white protein powder

- 3 tablespoons instant coffee powder
- 1/4 cup cacao powder
- 1/4 cup cacao nibs
- 5 tablespoons water

Instructions. Put parchment paper in an 8x8-inch square baking dish. Combine the coffee, egg white protein powder, cacao powder, and almonds in a food processor. The nuts should be processed until they are in very minute bits. Include the dates. Combining procedure. Add water, 1 tablespoon at a time, while processing, until a sticky consistency is reached. You need to take the processor's S-blade out. Chop up the cacao nibs and add them to the mixture. Put the liquid into the prepared square baking dish. Use a roller to make the mixture uniformly flat. Keep cold for at least 60 minutes. Separate into 16 pieces. Serve.

Nutrition Calories: 246 Kcal, Proteins: 12g, Fat: 12g, Carbohydrates: 19g

5.6 Carrot cake bites

Ingredients
- ½ cup rolled oats
- 1 cup walnut halves
- 2 tablespoons of flax seeds
- 1 grated carrot
- 2 tablespoons almond butter
- 1 teaspoon vanilla extract
- 2 teaspoons of cinnamon
- 2 tablespoons maple syrup
- Shredded coconut for rolling

Instructions. Gather the Ingredients and Supplies. Start by dividing the ingredients and gathering the supplies, such as the bowls, measuring cups, and the food processor. Add the base ingredients to a food processor. Add all ingredients except grated coconut to a food processor. Pulse the ingredients until you get a dough. Pulse until the mixture comes together, adding a small amount of water if necessary. Once the dough has formed, put it in the fridge for 15 minutes. Measure the dough into even bites. Once cooled, remove the dough from the fridge. Next, using a small spoon or tablespoon, measure the dough into even pieces.

Make Bite-Sized Balls. Next, make your Carrot Cake Power Bites from the dough. Plating and prepare the coconut topping. Once bite-sized balls are formed, add the coconut topping to a plate. Roll your bites in coconut. Now top off your energy bites by rolling the formed balls in the shredded coconut. Enjoy and save for later! Once you've added the ingredients, enjoy immediately or store them in an airtight container in the fridge for 3-4 days.

5.7 Autumn cocoa pudding and chai compote

Servings: 2

Ingredients

- 3 tbsp chia seeds
- 250 ml milk or vegetable drink
- 1 tsp soluble cocoa
- 1 pinch salt
- 4 apples
- Water
- 1/2 lemon (in juice)
- Spices (cardamom, cinnamon, cloves, pepper, ginger, nutmeg to taste)
- Natural organic yogurt without sugar
- Cashew cream

Instructions. Soak the chia seeds with milk, a pinch of salt, and cocoa. Let stand for at least 5 hours, so the seeds absorb all the liquid. For the compote, cut the apples, sprinkle them with spices to taste, and put them in the oven for 30 minutes or until you see that they are tender and have begun to release their delicious aroma. Beat the apples with lemon juice and a bit of water. Quite a lot of compote will come out, so you can save it for other recipes (it lasts a week in the fridge). Before assembling the pudding, stir the mixed chia seeds to prevent lumps from forming. Place the first layer of chia pudding on top of the compote and yogurt, and decorate with the cashew cream.

5.8 Grapefruit, ginger and turmeric lassi

Processing time: 10 minutes **Servings:** 1

Ingredients

- 250 ml of natural yogurt (it can be skimmed)
- 1/2 large grapefruit juice
- 1 piece of fresh ginger
- 1/2 teaspoon of ground turmeric
- a pinch of salt
- 1-2 tablespoons of honey or agave syrup taste
- a little water is needed.

Instructions. Wash the grapefruit, cut it in half and squeeze out the juice. We should get about half a glass of liquid. We can strain it to remove the pulp or leave it as is, ensuring no seeds have been strained. Cut a piece of ginger, depending on our tolerance for this product, peel and chop very finely, or grate using a suitable grater.

Place the yogurt with its whey, juice, ginger, turmeric, a small pinch of salt, and a tablespoon of honey in a blender or blender. Crush everything very well, mixing until you get a homogeneous texture without lumps. Taste and adjust the sweetness level to your liking by adding more honey. If it's too thick, add a little water or a little more juice. Serve immediately.

5.9 Sugar-free oatmeal and dried fruit cookies

Cooking: 15 minutes **Servings:** 20

Ingredients

- Eggs L two
- Shredded pumpkin 150g
- Ground cinnamon 2.5ml
- Vanilla 2.5ml
- Salt a bit
- Oatmeal 170g
- Chia seeds one teaspoon
- Flax seeds one teaspoon
- Raw almonds chopped, in sticks or sliced 50g
- Raisins 50g

Instructions. The recipe is as simple as mixing, forming, and baking. First, preheat the oven to 180°C and prepare one or two trays covering them with parchment paper or some non-stick material suitable for the oven. Place the eggs with the pumpkin, cinnamon, and vanilla in a medium bowl, and beat with a hand whisk until everything is well integrated. Add the salt, the oat flakes, the chia and flax seeds, and the almonds. Mix with a spatula or stick and add the raisins or larger chopped dried fruit at the end. Combine well to have a homogeneous dough and form cookies taking small portions with a few teaspoons. They form better if we take the dough with one and use the other, moistened, to deposit the portion. With wet fingers, we can finally give them a more rounded shape. We could also let the dough rest in the fridge for a few hours to cool down and thus form them with our hands more easily. They won't grow practically in the oven, so we can make them thicker if we want them tender inside or thinner if we want them crunchier. Sprinkle with a little cinnamon if desired, and bake for about 15-18 minutes or until browned to your liking. Wait a bit and let cool completely on a wire rack.

5.10 Tropical smoothie with turmeric

Servings: 1

Ingredients

- 1 cup frozen mango
- ½ cup fresh pineapple
- ⅓ cup coconut water
- 2 tablespoons plain Greek yogurt (unsweetened)
- ¼ teaspoon ground cinnamon
- ¼ teaspoon ground turmeric

Instructions. Cut the pineapple into small cubes. **Smoothie Preparation:** Place all ingredients in a high-powered blender.

Blend until all the ingredients are fully integrated and have a homogeneous consistency. **Tasting:** Once the tropical smoothie with turmeric is ready, you can add the topping of your choice; this time, I wanted to continue with the tropical wave and add a little dehydrated coconut.

5.11 Golden milk

Cooking: 10 minutes **Servings:** 2

Ingredients

- Milk or vegetable drink 500ml
- cinnamon stick 1
- Nails two
- green cardamom 1
- fresh ginger 5g
- black peppercorns two
- ground turmeric 5g
- Honey 15ml
- ground cinnamon to taste

Instructions. Heat the milk in a saucepan with the cinnamon stick, the cloves, the open cardamom, the peppercorns, and the chopped or ground ginger. Lower the heat before it reaches a boil, and add the turmeric, stirring well. Cook over very low heat for at least 5 minutes. Strain and add honey or a vegetable alternative to taste. Divide into cups and serve with a little ground cinnamon on top. It can also be whipped with a cappuccino mixer to make it fluffy or served with a cloud of milk.

5.12 Mango and banana smoothie bowl with seeds and red fruits

Servings: 1

Ingredients

- 1 small very ripe mango
- 1 ripe banana (half frozen and half natural)
- 2-4 tablespoons of plain yogurt
- 1 pinch of ground turmeric
- Lime or lemon juice
- 2 teaspoons of chia seeds
- 1 tablespoon of pumpkin seeds
- 1 teaspoon of peeled and chopped almonds
- 2 tablespoons of fresh or frozen berries.

Instructions. We can use the mango raw, or we can use it frozen. It is very practical to have portions of peeled and chopped ripe fruit in the freezer, especially mango, red fruits, pineapple, and banana. In any case, it should be very cold. The banana for this recipe can be frozen one hour before making it, reserving half in the fridge. Peel the mango and chop it, collecting the juices it releases. Puree in a blender, chopper, or food processor. Add the yogurt and blend a little more. Add half of the frozen banana and blend with the turmeric until it is incorporated into the base cream. Try and add lime or lemon juice or more yogurt as you like.

Mix well and arrange in a bowl that is not very flat. Complete by adding the rest of the peeled and sliced banana, chia seeds, pumpkin seeds, and red berries, which can be straight from the freezer. Finish with some almonds, which we can lightly toast in a frying pan without oil.

Tasting: The mango and banana smoothie bowl with seeds and berries should be served immediately, as this will retain all of its texture, and the extra ingredients will not become soggy. Other ingredients can be added, or some of those suggested can be substituted to taste, for example, with sesame seeds, walnuts or hazelnuts, a tablespoon of tahini, grated coconut, etc.

21 DAYS MEAL PLAN

DAY 1
Breakfast: Tigernut Waffles. Lunch: Tuna salad sandwich with side salad. Dinner: Poached salmon with rice and papaya. Snack: Greek yogurt with mixed berries

DAY 2
Breakfast: Fruit salad with nuts. Lunch: Almond crusted avocado and bulgur tomato salad. Dinner: Carrot tagliatelle with avocado pesto. Snack: Autumn cocoa pudding and chai compote

DAY 3
Breakfast: Bread with avocado and egg. Lunch: Fried sauerkraut with parsley quark. Dinner: Arugula Salad with Turmeric Cauliflower. Snack: Carrot cake bites

DAY 4
Breakfast: Cauliflower in cream cheese. Lunch: Baked fennel with caramelized grapes. Dinner: Beef and Ginger Skillet. Snack: Matcha latte and nut butter on whole grain toast

DAY 5
Breakfast: Chia Seed and Milk Pudding. Lunch: Spiced Lentil Soup. Dinner: False broccoli couscous with turmeric egg. Snack: Ginger Date Almond Bars

DAY 6
Breakfast: Tropical Smoothie Bowl. Lunch: Swiss Chard and Red Lentil Curried Soup. Dinner: Turkey Meatballs. Snack: Coffee Cacao Protein Bars

DAY 7
Breakfast: Anti-Inflammatory Salad. Lunch: Shrimp Garlic Zoodles. Dinner: Salmon papillote with leeks, ginger and teriyaki sauce. Snack: Ginger-Cinnamon Mixed Nuts

DAY 8
Breakfast: Apple Turkey Hash. Lunch: Kale Quinoa Shrimp Bowl. Dinner: Fennel and Courgette Cream With Vegetable Chips

DAY 9
Breakfast: Broccoli and Quinoa Breakfast Patties. Lunch: Herb omelette with smoked salmon. Dinner: Ratatouille. Snack: Autumn cocoa pudding and chai compote

DAY 10
Breakfast: Scrambled Tofu Breakfast Tacos. Lunch: Tomato Stew with Chickpea and Kale. Dinner: Bean Bolognese

DAY 11

Breakfast: Stuffed pineapple. Lunch: Rice bowl with chickpeas and cashew sauce. Dinner: Chinese Chicken Salad. Snack: Spicy Tuna Rolls

DAY 12

Breakfast: Almond porridge with blueberries. Lunch: Mediterranean One Pan Cod.
Dinner: Peppers Stuffed with Sweet Potato and Turkey

DAY 13

Breakfast: Almond porridge with blueberries. Lunch: Mediterranean One Pan Cod. Dinner: Peppers Stuffed with Sweet Potato and Turkey. Snack: Sugar-free oatmeal and dried fruit cookies

DAY 14

Breakfast: Spinach Fry Up & Tomato Mushroom. Lunch: Baked potatoes with broccoli. Dinner: Harissa and Chicken Tenders

DAY 15

Breakfast: Protein-Rich Turmeric Donuts. Lunch: Shrimp Fajitas. Dinner: Stir-Fried Snap Pea and Chicken. Snack: Carrot cake bites

DAY 16

Breakfast: Chia Seed and Milk Pudding. Lunch: Mediterranean One Pan Cod. Dinner: Arugula, quinoa and goat cheese salad

DAY 17

Breakfast: Smoothie Bowl with Raspberries. Lunch: Chicken and Greek Salad Wrap. Dinner: Peppers Stuffed with Sweet Potato and Turkey

DAY 18

Breakfast: Grass Strawberry Smoothie. Lunch: Kale Quinoa Shrimp Bowl. Dinner: Cauliflower and broccoli salad. Snack: Autumn cocoa pudding and chai compote

DAY 19

Breakfast: Peanut Butter and Banana Bread Granola. Lunch: Almond crusted avocado and bulgur tomato salad. Dinner: Turkey Burgers with Tzatziki Sauce. Snack: Greek yogurt with mixed berries

DAY 20

Breakfast: Cinnamon Granola with Fruits. Lunch: Orange Cardamom Quinoa with Carrots. Dinner: Kale and Sweet Potato Tostadas. Snack: Coffee Cacao Protein Bars

DAY 21

<u>Breakfast:</u> Avocado Grapefruit Salad with Quinoa. <u>Lunch:</u> Lemon Chicken with Quinoa Pepper Salad. <u>Dinner:</u> Chicken Chili and White Beans. <u>Snack:</u> Coffee Cacao Protein Bars

Conclusion

The healthiest diet plan is probably that of a plant-based eater. Vegetarians and vegans are sometimes stereotyped as weak or sickly, especially by meat eaters and those with a preference for cheap cuisine. These are only two examples of the "legend issuances" that people who aren't acquainted with vegetarianism or vegetarian cookery believe exist. Most of the veggies and other natural items that tend to make up a vegetarian's or vegan's diet are really rather nutrient dense and calorie light. Superior nutrition and positive health benefits, such as the reduced risk of cancer, heart disease, and diabetes type 2, are provided by anti-inflammatory diets. Vegetarians and vegans weigh around 35 pounds less than meat eaters, according to the second Adventist Health Study. It is crucial to know the truth and reject the falsehoods about the health advantages of eating foods that originate from the soil. There really are great advantages to consuming food that originates from the soil.

Made in the USA
Middletown, DE
29 April 2023